New York during the last Half Century.

Historical Discourse.

# New York during the last Half Century:

# A DISCOURSE

IN COMMEMORATION

OF

*The Fifty-third Anniversary*

OF THE

NEW YORK HISTORICAL SOCIETY,

AND OF

THE DEDICATION OF THEIR NEW EDIFICE,

(November 17, 1857.)

BY

JOHN W. FRANCIS, M. D., LL. D.

Fastigia Rerum.

NEW YORK:

JOHN F. TROW, PRINTER AND STEREOTYPER, 377 & 379 BROADWAY,

CORNER OF WHITE STREET.

1857.

# PREFACE.

It was considered desirable, on the occasion of inaugurating the new and beautiful edifice erected by the liberal contributions of the merchants and professional gentlemen of this city, for the permanent deposit of the manuscripts, books, and other property of the New York Historical Society, that the chief elements of civil and social development which have marked the annals of this metropolis, should be sketched in their origin and progress. As this could be most effectually done through personal reminiscences, the author of this brief historical record was chosen to perform the duty; partly because he is one of the few surviving early members of the Institution, and partly on account of the intimate relations he has sustained to many prominent citizens in all departments of life and vocation. Alive to the earnestly expressed wishes of his fellow-members, and cherishing a deep interest in the annals and prosperity of his native city, while he found the task accordant with his sympathies, he yet felt that the absorbing cares of an arduous profession were essentially opposed to the research and finish appropriate to such an enterprise; and he therefore craves the indulgence of his readers, as he did that of his audience. As delivered, this survey of New York in the past, was unavoidably curtailed; it is now presented as originally written.

The author cherishes the hope that it may be in his power, at a future time, to enlarge the record of local facts and individualities associated with the unprecedented growth of New York, since and immediately preceding the formation of her Historical Society. It will be seen that his aim has been to review the condition of the site, institutions, and character of our city during the last sixty years, and, in a measure, to trace their influence on its future prospects: as the commercial emporium of the Union and the seat of its most prosperous Historical Society, we have every reason to hope that our new and extensive arrangements will secure a large accession of valuable materials. Yet those members who bear in recollection the vast changes which have occurred within the period of our existence as an association, need not be told that the original landmarks and features of the metropolis have been either greatly modified or entirely destroyed; while carelessness, or the neglect of family memorials, renders it extremely difficult to reproduce, with vital interest, even the illustrious persons who have contributed most effectually to our prosperity and renown.

If the author succeeds, by means of the present brief sketch or a future more elaborate memoir, in awakening attention to the men and events which have secured the rapid development of resources on this island, both economical and social, he will rejoice. Such a task, rightly performed, should kindle anew our sense of personal responsibility as citizens, of gratitude as patriots, and of wise sympathy as scholars. Even this inadequate tribute he has regarded as an historical duty, and felt it to be a labor of love.

J. W. F.

New York, *November* 17, 1857.

*At a meeting of the NEW YORK HISTORICAL SOCIETY, held at the Library, on Tuesday evening, November* 17, 1857, *to celebrate the Fifty-Third Anniversary of the founding of the Society.*

Dr. John W. Francis delivered its Anniversary Address, entitled, "New York During the Last Half Century."

On its conclusion the Rev. Francis L. Hawks, D. D., after some remarks, submitted the following resolution:

*Resolved,* That the thanks of the Society be presented to Dr. Francis for his highly interesting address, and that a copy be requested for publication.

The resolution was seconded by Charles King, LL.D., and was then unanimously adopted.

Extract from the minutes.

ANDREW WARNER,

*Recording Secretary.*

---

ERRATA.

Page 107, line 29th, for 1787, read 1789.

Page 212, line 10th, for Rogers, read Moore.

Page 232, line 18th, for Oldest, read One of the oldest living members.

# DISCOURSE.

HONORED PRESIDENT AND ASSOCIATES OF THE NEW YORK HISTORICAL SOCIETY:

WHAT a contrast! This meeting of the New York Historical Society and that which was held now some fifty years ago. Ponder a while upon the circumstances which mark this difference. At the period at which our first organization took place, this city contained about sixty thousand inhabitants; at present it embraces some seven hundred and fifty thousand inhabitants. A large majority of the residents dwelt below Courtland street and Maiden Lane. A sparse population then occupied that portion of the island which lies above the site of the New York Hospital on Broadway; and the grounds now covered with the magnificent edifices which ornament Upper Broadway, the Fifth Avenue, Fourteenth Street, Union Place, and Madison Square, were graced with the sycamore, the elm, the oak, the chestnut, the wild cherry, the peach, the pear, and the plum tree, and further ornamented with gardens appropriated to horticultural products, with here and there the artichoke, the tulip, and the sun-flower. Where now stands our Astor Library, the New York Medical College, the Academy of Music, Cooper's Institute, and the Bible Society

House, the old gardens of our Dutch ancestors were most abundant, cultivated with something of the artistic regularity of the Hollanders, luxuriating in the sweet marjoram, the mint, the thyme, the currant, and the gooseberry. The banks of our majestic rivers on either side presented deep and abrupt declivities, and the waters adjacent were devoted to the safety of floating timber, brought down from the Mohawk, on the Hudson River, or elsewhere obtained, on the Connecticut, in mighty rafts, destined for naval architecture and house-building. Our avenues, and squares, and leading roads were not yet laid out by Morris, and Clinton, and Rutherford, and our street regulations in paving and sidewalks, even in those passes or highways now most populous, had reached but little above the Park, and in the Bowery only within the precincts of Bayard street. The present City Hall was in a state of erection, and so circumscribed, at that time, was the idea of the City's progress, that the Common Council, by a slender majority, after serious discussion, for economy's sake, decided that the postern part of the Hall should be composed of red-stone, inasmuch as it was not likely to attract much notice from the scattered inhabitants who might reside above Chambers street.

Some fifty years ago the most conspicuous of the residences of our prominent citizens were the Government House at the Bowling Green, the Kennedy House, now converted into the Washington Hotel, No. 1 Broadway, an object of singular interest. During the Revolution it was occupied by Howe and Clinton. Here Andrè commenced his correspondence with Arnold; and here John Pintard held an interesting conversation with Andrè on their respective claims to

Huguenot blood. Captain Peter Warren, who erected this famous building, was afterwards knighted, and became a Member of Parliament. The house was long occupied by Kennedy, afterwards Earl of Cassilis, and again by Sir Henry Clinton; afterwards it was long held by Nathaniel Prime, of the banking house of Prime & Ward. We next, in those earlier days, observe the stone dwelling, situated at the lower part of Broadway, once occupied by Governor Jay; the mansion of Governor George Clinton, of revolutionary renown, situated near the North River, at the termination of Thirteenth street, Colonel Rutgers' somewhat sequestered retreat, near the head of Cherry street, where Franklin sometimes took a patriotic meal; the Hero of Fort Stanwix, Colonel Willett's humble cottage in the vicinity; General Gates' ample establishment higher up near Twenty-fourth street, overlooking the banks of the East River, where Baron Steuben, Colonel Burr, and many other actors of the War, participated in the festivities so amply provided by the guest, with song and sentiment. The famous Club of the Belvidere, on the banks of the East River, is also entitled to commemoration: at its head was Atchisen: here royalty and democracy had their alternate revelries, with blessings on the king or laudations of the rights of man. Still standing, in pride of early state, we notice the Beekman House, near Fiftieth street, also near the East River banks, where British Officers rendezvoused, in revolutionary times; where Sir William Howe kept those vigils commemorated in the Battle of the Kegs, and where Andrè passed his last night previous to entering on his disastrous mission. Adjacent the Beekman House recently stood the ample

Green House, where Nathan Hale, called the spy, was examined by Lord Howe.

Eminently conspicuous in former days was the Mansion, located on Richmond Hill, near Lispenard's Meadows, at the junction of Varick and Van Dam streets, then an elevated and commanding sight. So many now before me must retain a strong recollection of this spot, which afterwards became the Theatre of the Montressor Opera Company, that I am compelled to dwell a moment longer concerning it. This imposing edifice was built about 1770, by Mortier, a paymaster of the British government. It was surrounded by many and beautiful forest trees; it was often subjected to the annoyances of the sportsmen, and Mr. Van Wagenen, a direct descendant of Garret Van Wagenen, almost the first and earliest of our city schoolmasters, a true son of St. Nicholas, still honoring us in his life and in his devotion to New York, could give you a curious account of the enjoyments of the field on these premises in those early days. While Congress sat in this city, this celebrated mansion was occupied by the elder Adams, and some of the most charming letters of the Vice President's wife are dated at this place. It subsequently became the residence of Aaron Burr, into whose possession it fell, by purchase from the executors of Abraham Mortier; in 1804 it became by purchase the property of John Jacob Astor. While Burr resided there, its halls occasionally resounded with the merriment which generous cheer inspires; yet at other times, and more frequently, philosophy here sat enthroned amidst her worshippers. Here Talleyrand, who in the morning had discoursed on the tariff with Hamilton, passed perhaps the afternoon of the same day with Burr, on the subject of the fur trade and commerce with Great Britain, associated with Volney, whose portly form gave outward tokens of his tremendous gastric powers, while the Syrian traveller, in his turn, descanted on theogony, the races of the red men, and Niagara. I cannot well conceive of a greater intellectual trio. Perhaps it was at one of those convivial entertainments that the dietetic sentiment originated, in relation to some of the social peculiarities among us, that our Republic, while she could boast of some two hundred varieties of religious creeds, possessed only one variety of gravy.

Here it may be recorded lived Burr, at the time of the fatal duel with Hamilton: informed by his sagacious second, Van Ness, that the General was wounded, Burr remarked, "O, the little fellow only feigns hurt," but catching an idea of the nature of the wound, from Hamilton's action, he hastily left the field, and fled for shelter from the wrath of an indignant people, while rumor spread that the constituted authorities were in search of him. It was believed by the populace that he had passed through New Jersey towards the South, yet on the very afternoon of that fatal day, while the whole city was in consternation, and on the look-out, he had already reached his domicile on Richmond Hill, and was luxuriating in his wonted bath, with Rousseau's Confessions in his hands, for his mental sustenance.

But I proceed with these hasty notices of our city in these earlier times, about the period when the organization and establishment of the Historical Society were contemplated, and about to be incorporated by legislative wisdom.

Our City Library was now in possession of its new structure in Nassau street, and justly boasted of its rare and valuable treasures, its local documents of importance, and its learned librarian, John Forbes. Kent's Hotel, on Broad street, was the great rendezvous for heroic discussions on law and government, and for political and other meetings; and here the great Hamilton was at times the oracle of the evening. The City Hotel, near old Trinity, was the chosen place for the Graces; here Terpsichore presided, with her smiling countenance, and Euterpe first patronized Italian music in this country, under the accomplished discipline of Trazzata. This long known and ample hall is not to be forgotten as the first building in this city, if not in this country, in which slate was used as a roof-covering, thus supplanting the old Dutch tile of the Hollanders, in use from the beginning of their dynasty among us.

Our museums were limited to the one kept by old Gardener Baker, himself and his collection, a sort of curiosity shop, composed of heterogeneous fragments of the several kingdoms of nature. Hither childish ignorance was sometimes lost in wonder, and here too was the philosopher occasionally enlightened. Scudder did not lay the foundation of his patriotic enterprise until five years after our incorporation, and although his beginning was but an humble demonstration, he astounded the natives with his vast tortoise, and Alexander Wilson, the ornithologist, gave him cheering counsel, and enkindled his zeal. Our famous Vauxhall Garden of these earlier days, occupied the wide domain of the Bayards, situated on the left of our then Bunker Hill, near Bullock, now Broome street, and here the Osage Indians, amidst fireworks of dazzling efficacy (for we had not the use of calium nor strontium in these artistic displays in those days), yelled the war-whoop and danced the war-dance, while our learned Dr. Mitchill, often present on these occasions, translated their songs for the advancement of Indian literature, and enriched the journals with ethnological science concerning our primitive inhabitants.

The Indian Queen and Tyler's were gardens of much resort, situated towards the Greenwich side of our city: at the former military evolutions were often displayed to the satisfaction of the famous French general, Moreau, with General Stevens and Morton among the staff as official inspectors, while Tyler's is still held in remembrance, by some few surviving graduates of Columbia College, as the resort for commencement suppers. I shall advert to only one other site, which, though in days gone by not a public garden, was a place much frequented. On the old road towards Kingsbridge, on the eastern side of the island, was the well-known Kip's Farm, pre-eminently distinguished for its grateful fruits, the plum, the peach, the pear, and the apple, and for its choice culture of the *rosaceæ*. Here the *êlite* often repaired as did good old Dr. Johnson and Boswell for recreation at Ranelagh; and here our Washington, now invested with presidential honors, made an excursion, and was presented with the Rosa Gallica, an exotic first introduced into this country in this garden; fit emblem of that memorable union of France and the American colonies in the cause of republican freedom. These three gardens were famous for their exquisite fruit, the plum, and the peach: equally as are Newtown and Blackwell Island for the apple, known to all horticulturists, abroad and at home, as the Newtown pippin. Such things were. No traces are now to be found of the scenes of those once gratifying sights; the havoc of progressive improvement has left nought of these once fertile gardens of Dutch regularity, save the old pear tree of the farm of the redoubtable Peter Stuveysant, well known as still flourishing in foliage and in fruit, in its 220th year, at the corner of Thirteenth street and Third Avenue. If tradition be true, the biographer of this venerable tree, in his account, in the London Horticultural Transactions, ought not to have omitted the curious fact, that of its importation from Southern Europe, and of its having once occupied the old fort held by Stuyvesant and delineated by Vander Donck. If all this be authentic, the old pear tree enhances our admiration as the last living thing in existence since the time of the Dutch Dynasty.

Order demands that our first notice of the most striking of our ornamental grounds should be an account of the Battery, and its historical associate, White Hall. Few, perhaps, are well informed of the origin of that well recorded name, and long-lived historical location. John Moore, the last on the list of the members of the "Social Club," died in New York in 1828, in his 84th year. He was a grandson of Colonel John Moore, who was an eminent merchant of this city, and one of the Aldermen, when it was a great distinction to possess that honor: he was also a member of his Majesty's Provincial Council at the time of his death, in 1749. The Colonel resided at the corner of Moore (so called after his demise by the corporation) and Front streets, in the largest and most costly house in this city at that time, and called "White Hall" from its color, and which gave the name afterwards to the neighboring street. It is scarcely necessary to add, that this great edifice was destroyed by the fire which laid waste the city in September, 1776, three days after the British obtained possession of it. Of the Bay and harbor, and of the Battery itself, I need say nothing after the successful description of Mrs. Trollope, and many other writers. The first time I entered that charming place, was on the occasion of the funeral of General Washington. The procession gathered there, and about the Bowling Green: the Battery was profusely set out with the Lombardy poplar trees: indeed in 1800–'4 and '5 they infested the whole island, if not most of the middle, northern, and many southern States. Their introduction was curious. The elder Michaux, under the direction of Louis XVI., had been sent to America, from the Garden of Plants of Paris: he brought out with him the gardener, Paul Saunier, who possessed, shortly after, horticultural grounds of some extent in New Jersey. The Lombardy tree promised everything good, and Paul spread it. It was pronounced an exotic of priceless value; but like many things of an exotic nature, it polluted the soil, vitiated our own more stately and valuable indigenous products: and at length we find that American sagacity has proscribed its growth, and is daily eradicating it as uncongenial and detrimental to the native riches of American husbandry.

In glancing at other beautiful plots, if I am controlled by the definition of the dictionary, I must omit special mention of that once famous spot of ground called the Park, situated in front of our City Hall, inasmuch as artistic taste and corporation sacrilege caused the cutting down of the more conspicuous and beautiful trees, the sycamores, the maple, the walnut, and the Babylonian willows of the growth of ages, which constituted its woodland, in order to favor the populace with an improved view of the architectural front of our then recently erected marble edifice. In its actual condition (lucus non lucendo) it were too latitudinarian to speak of the Old Commons as a park, at the present day. Yet the Liberty Boys have perpetuated it in our early history, and Clinton's Canal has given it a modern glorification, by the far-famed meeting of the tens of thousands at which the venerable Colonel Few presided, to enter their protest against legislative proscription in 1824.

At the period to which our associations are mainly confined, Washington square, which a wise forethought of our city fathers some time since converted into an eligible park, was not then contemplated. It is known to you all to have been our Golgotha during the dreadful visitations of the Yellow Fever in 1797, 1798, 1801, and 1803, and many a victim of the pestilence of prominent celebrity, was consigned to that final resting-place on earth, regardless of his massive gains, or his public services. I shall only specify one individual whose humble tombstone was the last of the sepulchral ornaments removed thence: I allude to Doctor Benjamin Perkins, the inventor of the metallic tractors, a charlatan, whose mesmeric delusions, like clairvoyance in these our own days, had something of a popular recognition, and whose confidence and temerity in the treatment of his case, yellow fever, by his own specific, terminated in his death, after three days' illness. St. John's Park, now richly entitled to that designation from the philosophy of the vegetable economy which was evinced at its laying-out, in the selection, association, and distribution of its trees, by the late Louis Simond, the distinguished traveller, (for the vegetable as well as the animal kingdom has its adjuvants, its loves, and its hatreds,) had no existence at the time to which we more directly refer, the period of our incorporation. If a botanical inquirer should investigate the variety of trees which flourish in the St. John's Park, he would most likely find a greater number than on any other ground, of equal size, in the known world. If what everybody says be true, then is Samuel B. Ruggles entitled to the meed of approbation from every inhabitant of this metropolis, for the advantageous disposition of the Union Place Park, and its adjacent neighborhood. It was the lot of this enterprising citizen to manifest an enlarged forecast during his public career in municipal, equally effective as he had evinced in State affairs.

The equestrian statue of Washington, executed with artistic ability by Brown, and erected in this square through the patriotic efforts of Col. Lee, aided by our liberal merchants, adds grace to the beauty of that open thoroughfare of the city. There is a story on this subject, which, I hope, will find embodiment in some future edition of Joe Miller. Col. Lee had assiduously collected a subscription for this successful statue; among others, towards the close of his labors, he honored an affluent citizen of the neighborhood, by an application for aid in the goodly design. "There is no need of the statue," exclaimed the votary of wealth: "Washington needs no statue; he lives in the hearts of his countrymen; that is his statue." "Ah! indeed," replied the colonel, "does he live in yours?" "Truly, he does," was the reply. "Then," added the colonel, "I am sorry, very sorry, that he occupies so mean a tenement."

I trust I am not vulnerable to the charge of diverging too far from an even path, into every field that may skirt the road, if while on the subject of Gardens and Parks, I commemorate one other of superior claims to consideration, and which at the time we have so often alluded to, had arrived to a degree of importance which might almost be called national; I mean the Elgin Botanic Garden, founded by the late Dr. David Hosack, in 1801, and at the period of our incorporation, justly pronounced an object of deep interest to the cultivators of natural knowledge, and to the curious in vegetable science. Those twenty acres of culture, more or less, were a triumph of individual zeal, ambition, and liberality, of which our citizens had reason to be proud, whether they deemed the garden as conservative of our indigenous botany, or as a repository of the most precious exotics. The eminent projector of this distinguished garden, with a princely munificence, had made these grounds a resort for the admirers of nature's vegetable wonders, and for the students of her mysteries. Here were associated, in appropriate soil, exposed to the native elements, or protected by the conservatory and the hot-house, examples of vegetable life, and of variety of development—a collection that might have captivated a Linnæus, or a Jussieu; and here, indeed, a Michaux, and a Barton, a Mitchill, a Doughty, a Pursh, a Wilson, or a Leconte, often repaired to solve the doubts of the cryptogamist, or to confirm the nuptial theory of Vaillant.*

* Several of these distinguished disciples of the school of wisdom have already found judicious biographers, who have recorded their services in the fields of natural knowledge. We still want the pen to describe the labors of Pursh, the author of the Flora Americæ Septentrionalis. His

Here the learned Hosack, then Professor of Botany in Columbia College, gave illustrations to his medical class, and to many not exactly within the circle of professional life, of the naturàl and artificial systems of nature. I shall never forget those earlier days of my juvenile studies, when the loves and habits of plants and of trees were first expounded by that lucid instructor, and with what increased delight the treasures of the Jardin des Plantes of Paris, just arrived, through the kindness of Monsieur Thouin, were added to the

adventurous spirit, his hazardous daring, and his indomitable energy, present an example of what a devotee in an attached calling will encounter. He was for several years the curator of the Elgin Botanic Garden, and widely travelled through the United States. Lambert, the author of the "American Pines," afforded him great aid in the production of his volumes, and cherished, as I personally know, great regard for the benefits Pursh had conferred on American botany. Michaux has been more fortunate. The biographical memoir of this most eminent man, recently given to the public in the "Transactions of the American Philosophical Society," by Elias Durand, of Philadelphia, himself a lover of botanical science, is a most grateful tribute to the character and merits of this intrepid explorer of the American soil. Michaux was the only child of André Michaux, rendered no less famous by his "Oaks of North America," and by his "Flora," than the son by his "Forest Trees." Young Michaux, under parental guidance, was early initiated into the cultivation of botanical pursuits; the story of his life, as given us by Mr. Durand, enhances our esteem of his heroic labors, and posterity must ever thank this enlightened biographer for the exposition he has made of the contributions to physical knowledge, and especially to arboriculture, which the instrumentality of Michaux has effected. He lived a long life, notwithstanding his innumerable perils, dying so late as in October, 1855, at the age of 85 years. Every American who visits the Garden of Plants of Paris, must be struck with the number and the richness of the American Forest Trees which flourish therein; they furnish but one of many examples of the practical zeal and services of the Michauxs, father and son. It is to be hoped that, ere long, some competent botanist will favor us with an account of the amiable Douglass, whose tragical end is still involved in obscurity. We know little of him save that our botanical catalogue is enriched with the "Pinus Douglasii." Greater merits, and more modesty, were never blended in one individual.

great collection of exotics in this New York Garden. It was a general rule with that able instructor to terminate his spring course by a strawberry festival. "I must let the class see," said the teacher, "that we are practical as well as theoretical: the fragaria is a most appropriate aliment: Linnæus cured his gout and protracted his life by strawberries." "They are a dear article," I observed, "to gratify the appetite of so many." "Yes, indeed," he rejoined, "but in due time, from our present method of culture, they will become abundant and cheap. The disciples of the illustrious Swede must have a foretaste of them, if they cost me a dollar a piece."

Had Dr. Hosack done no more by his efforts at the Elgin Garden, than awaken increased desires in the breast of his pupil Torrey for natural knowledge, he might be acknowledged a public benefactor, from the subsequent brilliant career which that eminent naturalist, with Professor Gray, has pursued in the vast domain of botanical inquiry. But I am happy to add, with that social impulse which seems to be implanted in the breast of every student of nature, which the frosts of eighty-eight winters had not chilled in Antoine Jusseau, and which glowed with equal benignity in the bosom of the intrepid Ledyard, on Afric's sandy plains, and in the very heart of the adventurous Kane amidst the icy poles, Hosack is not forgotten. Willdenow tells us, that the crowning glory of the botanist is to be designated by some plant bearing his name. Since the death of Dr. Hosack, the botanical nomenclature enrols no less than sixteen species of plants of different regions under the genus *Hosackia.* Time and circumstances have wrought great changes in this once celebrated place, the Elgin Garden.

Columbia College, that venerable and venerated seat of classical learning, was justly proud of her healthy and beautiful locality, laved almost up to the borders of her foundation by the flowing streams of the Hudson, and ornamented by those majestic sycamores planted by the Crugers, the Murrays, and the Jays, fifty years before our incorporation, but which city progress has recently so agonizingly rooted out. Well might Cowen, in his Tractate on Education, have extolled this once delectable spot as an appropriate seat for intellectual culture in the New World.

As a graduate for nearly half a century, an overweening diffidence must not withhold from me the trespass of a moment concerning my Alma Mater. The faculty, when I entered within its walls, was the same as occupied them when our Historical Society was organized, and on a former occasion, at one of your anniversaries, I bore testimony to the cordial support which that body gave to our institution at its inception. The benignant Bishop Moore was its president; Dr. Kemp, a strong mathematician, ably filled several departments of science; impulsive and domineering in his nature, there were moments with him when a latent benevolence towards the student quickened itself, and he may be pronounced to have been an effective teacher. It has been promulgated that he gave early hints of the practicability of the formation of the Erie Canal. I have never seen satisfactory proofs of such forethought in any of his disquisitions. He died shortly after that great measure was agitated: he might have conversed on the subject with Clinton, Morris, Eddy, Colles and Fulton. Yet I think I might, with perhaps equal propriety, because I had an interview with old

William Herschel, fancy myself a discoverer of the nature of the milky way. Kemp was clever in his assigned duties, but had little ambition to tract beyond it. He was devoid of genius and lacked enterprise.

Dr. Bowden, as the Professor of Moral Philosophy, was a courteous gentleman, a refined scholar and a belles-lettres writer. Like many others of a similar type, his controversial pen carried pungency with its ink, while in personal contact with his opponents, his cautious and modulated utterance neither ruffled the temper nor invoked vehemence in reply. Professor M'Vickar, so long his successor, has given the life and character of this excellent man with graphic accuracy, and our late departed and much lamented associate, Ogden Hoffman, has furnished a portrait of his virtues in an occasional address with the fidelity and attractiveness of the limner's art.

Our Professor of the Greek and Latin tongues, was the late Dr. Wilson: he enjoyed through a long life the reputation of a scholar; he was a devoted man to his calling, and a reader of wide extent. His earnestness in imparting knowledge was unabated through a long career, and had his intellectual texture been more plastic, he had proved himself to his scholars a triumphant expositor. He seemed to want the discipline of a more refined and general scholarship; at times harassed in his classical exegesis, he became the veriest pedagogue, and his derivative theory and verbal criticism, were often provocatives of the loudest laughter. The sublimity of Longinus was beyond his grasp, and he only betrayed his hardihood when he attempted to unfold the beauties of the Sapphic Ode. He was enamored of Josephus, and recreated in the history of that ancient people of Israel; so much so as to enter with warmth into measures the better to secure their spiritual salvation; and if the newspapers, often our best authority, are to be relied on, associated himself with a Society for the Conversion of the Jews; and it is affirmed, he secured, after years of effort, one at least within the sheepfold of Calvinistic divinity. Dr. Wilson, though cramped with dactyls and spondees, was generous in his nature, of kindly feelings, and of great forbearance towards his pupils. Few of our American colleges have enjoyed the blessings of so earnest a teacher for so long a term of years; and the occurrence is still rarer, that so conscientious a professor has been followed by a successor of at least equal zeal in his classical department, and who is still further enriched with the products of advanced philology and critical taste.*

Columbia College has seen her centurial course. While I feel that that noticeable asterisk prefixed to the names of her departed sons will ere long mark my own, I cannot but recognize the renown she has acquired from the men of thought and action whom she has sent forth to enrich the nation. Let us award her the highest praises for the past, while we indulge the fondest hopes for the future, and a great future lies before her. The eminent men who have successively presided over her government, from her first Johnson to her present distinguished head, Dr. King, have uniformly enforced with a fixed determination, classical and mathematical acquisitions, without which a retrograde movement in intellectual discipline and in practical

* Charles Anthon, LL.D.

pursuits must take place. While I accede to this indubitable truth, I may prove sceptical of the often repeated assertion of my old master, Wilson, that without the classics you can neither roast a potato nor fly a kite. It is currently reported that the fiscal powers of Columbia College are more commanding than ever; hence the duty becomes imperative, to enlarge her portals of wisdom in obedience to the spirit of the age. Let her proclaim and confirm the riches of classic lore; let its culture, by her example, become more and more prevalent. Her statutes assure us she spreads a noble banquet for her guests; but, disclaiming the monitorial, let her bear in mind the sanitory precept of the dietetist, that variety of aliment is imperative for the full development of the normal condition. The apician dishes of the ancients did not always prove condimental, and the rising glory of an independent people, not yet of her own age, has needs and seeks relief in the acquisition of new pursuits, and in the exercise of new thoughts corresponding with the novelty of their condition and the wants of the republic.

I had written thus much concerning my venerable Alma Mater, and was content to leave her in the enjoyment of that repose, if so she desired, which revolving years had not disturbed, when lo! popular report and the public journals announce that new life has entered into her constitution. The lethargy which so long oppressed her, she has thrown off; she has found relief in the quickened spirit of the times, and in the doings of those intellectual bodies which surround her, and which modern science has called into being. Let me, an humble individual, venture to give her the assurances of a mighty population, in whose midst she stands, that the learned and the enlightened, the honest and the true, of every quarter, hail her advent in unmeasured accents of praise. In the moral, in the scholastic, in the scientific world, her friends rise up to greet her with warmest approbation; there are already manifested throughout the land outward and visible signs of joy at her late movements, and her alumni everywhere cherish an inward and genuine rejoicing at anticipated benefits. She has found out by the best of teachers, experience, that apathy yields not nutrition; that there is a conservatism which is more liable to destroy than to protect. From Aristotle down to the present time, the schoolmen have affirmed that laughter is the property of reason, while the excess of it has been considered as the mark of folly. It needs no cart team to draw the parallel. Liberated by the increased wisdom of the age, she now comes forth in new proportions, and puts on the habiliments of one conscious that her armor is fitted for the strongest contest, and ready to enter the field of competition with the most heroic of her compeers. The desire on all sides to extend the empire of knowledge, opens the widest area for her operations, and that great educational test, sound, practical, and available instruction, we feel assured her richly endowed board of professors fully comprehend, the better to rear up the moral and intellectual greatness of the American nation.

More than two centuries ago, Milton, in strong accents, told the world, in his tractate on education, when referring to the physical sciences, that "the linguist, who should pride himself to have all the tongues that Babel cleft the world into, yet if he have not studied the solid things in them as well as the words and lexicons, he were nothing so much to be esteemed a learned man, as any yeoman or tradesman completely wise in his mother's dialect." Yet ages have rolled on since this oracular declaration, while the monition of this great scholar has passed by unheeded. But Oxford now knows that languages alone will not save her, though aided by Aristotle, and Cambridge has found that more than the calculus is demanded at her hands.

I have repeatedly listened to the verbal remarks of those two illustrious graduates of old Columbia, Gouverneur Morris and De Witt Clinton, on the subjects most important in a course of collegiate instruction for the youth of this country. Morris urged, with his full, flowing periods, the statesman's science, government and the American constitution; Clinton was tenacious of the physical and mechanical sciences: both concurred in opinion that a professorship of cookery was indispensable to secure health and longevity to the people. But these philosophers had only recently returned from their exploratory tour to the west, as canal commissioners, to decide upon the route for the Erie Canal, and, as I conjecture, must have fared indifferently at that time in their journey through that almost untrodden wilderness.

From the period when the Abbé Haüy unfolded the theory of chrystallography, we may date the introduction, in a liberal way, of the physical branches of science in academies and universities; and with the chart of Bacon's outlines ever before us, the mighty fact of Milton is best understood, that acquaintance with things around us will best enable us to comprehend things above us; thus studying the visible, the better to learn and admire the invisible. What, then, is to be the nature of the intellectual repast a collegiate system is to set before its scholars, seeing great diversity of sentiment prevails. The spirit of the times declares it, and a vast and rising republic demands it. Let the classics be not shorn of their proper dimensions, and in the discipline of her Anthon and her Drisler, they will neither lose symmetry, nor become amorphous. Let geometry and her kindred branches prefer her claims to consideration by her erudite Hackley, and her adjunct, the renowned Davies, of West Point celebrity: let natural philosophy and that science which seems to inosculate with almost every other, chemistry, be developed in all their relations by those ardent disciples, McCulloh and Joy: let that adept in teaching, her recently elected Leiber, expound constitutional law and public and private rights; and while God and nature have established an eternal difference between things profane and things holy, let the fountain be ever open from which flows that wisdom imparted by your venerable instructor, McVickar, for the benefit of ingenuous youth in all after life.

In the range of human pursuits, there is no avocation so grateful to the feelings as that of unfolding wisdom to generous and susceptible youth: philosophy to the mind is as assuredly nutriment to the soul, as poison must prove baneful to the animal functions. Whatever may be the toil of the instructor, who can calculate his returns? In the exercise of his great prerogative, he is decorating the temple of the immortal mind; he is refining the affections of the human heart. Old Columbia, with her fiscal powers, adequate to every emergency, with the rich experience of a century, with the proud roll of eminent sons whom she has reared, and who have exerted an influence on the literature and destinies of the commonwealth; these, without the enumeration of other concurring circumstances, are enough to encourage comprehensive views of blessings in store: and that heart and head will co-operate effectively in the reformation of abuses which time had almost made venerable, and delight in the glorious undertaking, fortified in the councils of a benignant Providence, of rearing to full stature a University commensurate with the enlarged policy that characterizes New York, is the prayer of this generation, and cannot fail to be of the future, to whom its perpetuity is bequeathed.

There are few of my auditory who have not been struck with the increase, both in numbers and in architectural display, of our ecclesiastical edifices. When this Society was an applicant for incorporation, the Roman Catholic denomination had one place of worship, situated in Barclay street, and organized in 1786: they now have thirty-nine. The Jews of the Portuguese order, the victims of early intolerance by the inquisition of Portugal, and who first came among us prior to the time of old Gov. Stuyvesant, had but one synagogue for upwards of a century, situated in Mill street: they now have eighteen. The Episcopal denomination had seven churches, they now have forty-nine. The Baptists had three, they now boast thirty. But I can proceed no further in these details. When I published an account of New York and its institutions in 1832,* we had one hundred and twenty-three places of public worship: our aggregate at this time

* Brewster's Edinburgh Encyclopædia.

approaches three hundred, of which we may state that sixty are of the Dutch Reformed and Presbyterian denominations, and forty of the Methodists. As I dismiss the churches, I am also compelled to omit almost all notice of the departed worthies of the various denominations with whom I have been personally acquainted, or heard as pastors of their several flocks. Our worthy founder, John Pintard, was extremely solicitous that we should give minute attention to the American church, and preserve faithful records of her progress. Had we labored severely in this species of inquiry we might have had much to do, and I fear have proved derelict in many things, which, as a Historical Society, called louder on our time and for our devotion.

Early instruction and reading while a boy, gave me something of a bias towards matters pertaining to churches and their pastors: my repeated visits to my father's grave, in Ann street, when I was not yet seven years old, led me to church yards and to epitaphs, and I had collected, when scarcely able to pen an intelligible hand, quite a volume of those expressive memorials of saddest bereavement. I state these facts, lest in what I have to say, in a brief notice of a few of the earlier clerical worthies of this city, you might apprehend, from my personal reminiscences, that I was half a century older than I actually am.

Christopher C. Kunze was the first clergyman I ever cast eyes upon. He was of the Evangelical German Lutheran Church. He officiated in the old stone edifice corner of Frankfort and William streets; he was the successor of Muhlenburg, who afterwards was the president of the convention that ratified the Constitution, and speaker of the House of Representatives. His political career is rendered memorable by his casting vote in behalf of Jay's treaty. As little is said of Kunze in the books, I may state, that he was a native of Saxony, was born in 1744, educated at the Halle Orphan House, and studied theology at the University of that city. Thence he was called in 1771 to the service of the Lutheran churches St. Michael and Zion's in Philadelphia. In 1784 he accepted a call from the Evangelical Lutheran church in William, corner of Frankfort street, as stated. Here he officiated until his death in 1807. He held the professorship of Oriental languages in Columbia College, from 1784 to 1787, and from 1792 to 1795. While Kunze occupied his ecclesiastical trust, a struggle arose to do away the German and substitute the English language in preaching. With assistance, Dr. Kunze prepared a collection of Hymns, translated into English: they were the most singular specimens of couplets and triplets I ever perused, yet they possessed much of the intensity and spiritualism of German poetry. This was in the fall of 1795.* Dr. Kunze was a scholar somewhat after the order of old Dr. Styles, and deeply versed in the fathers, in theology. He was so abstracted from worldly concerns and the living manners of the times, that like Jackey Barrett, of Trinity College, Dublin, he practically scarcely knew a sheep from a goat, though he might have quoted to your satisfaction Virgil and Tibullus. He reared the moral and intellectual structure of Henry Stuber, who wrote the Continuance of the life of Franklin, and who then sunk into

* Published by Hurtin & Commardinger. New York: John Tiebout: 12mo, 1795.

the grave by an insidious consumption. Kunze was versed in astronomy, and was something of an astrologer. He was quite skilled in numismatics, and you can appreciate the value of the rich collection of medals and coins which his family placed at the disposal of our Society. Kunze died fifty years ago, and in his death we lost one of our great scholars, and a worthy man. He held a newspaper controversy on the Gregorian period of the century 1800, and published a Sermon entitled "King Solomon's great sacrifice," delivered at the dedication of the English Lutheran Zion Church, October 4, 1801. It demonstrates his command of the English language.

There is associated with this movement of the English Hymn Book for the Lutheran church, a transaction which can hardly be overlooked. It is connected with our literary history. The increase of our native population, after the war, produced an increased demand for tuition as well as for preaching in the English tongue, and while the Lutheran Cathecism found a translator in the Rev. George Strebeck and Luther's black-letter Bible yielded to James's, (the English,) the German Theatre, with Kotzebue at its head, was now beginning to find among us readers, and actors in an English dress, and William Dunlap and Charles Smith, a bookseller in Pearl street, (afterwards better known for his valuable Military Repository, on the American Revolution,) and the Rev. H. P. Will, furnished materials for the acting drama from this German source, for the John street theatre; so that in New York we had a foretaste of Kotzebue and Schiller ere they were subjected to the criticism of a London audience, or were embodied in Thompson's translations of the German Theatre.

It was just about this period that Dominie Johannes Daniel Gros, a preacher of the Reformed Dutch Church of Nassau street, (where Gen. North erected a beautiful mural tablet to Baron Steuben,) having discoursed both in the German and English tongues, retired from the field of his labors, left the city, and settled at Canandaigua, where he died in 1812. His praises were on every lip, and here and there is still a living graduate of Columbia College who will tell you how, under those once ornamental buttonwoods, he drilled his collegiate class on Moral Philosophy, while the refined and classical Cochran (like our Anthon of these days) unfolded the riches of the Georgics, and Kemp labored to excite into action his electrical apparatus. The last of our theological worthies who used the language of Holland in the ministry, was the Rev. Dr. Gerardus Kuypers, of the Dutch Reformed Church. He died in 1833. But I forbear to trespass upon the interesting Memorial of the Dutch Church recently published by our learned Vice-President, Dr. De Witt.*

I was well acquainted with Joseph Pilmore and Francis Asbury: the former, with Boardman, the first regular itinerant preachers of this country, sent out by John Wesley: Pilmore was a stentorian orator. The latter, Asbury, was delegated as general superintendent of the Society's interest, and was afterwards denominated Bishop: they were most laborious and devoted men, mighty travellers through the American wilds in

* See that valuable record, "A Discourse delivered in the North Reformed Dutch Church, (Collegiate,) in the city of New York, on the last Sabbath in August, 1856. By Thomas De Witt, D. D., one of the Ministers of the Collegiate Reformed Dutch Church. New York, 1857.

the days of Oglethorpe. Pilmore finally took shelter in the doctrines of episcopacy. Asbury was by no means an uproarious preacher. A second Whitfield in his activity, in his locomotive faculty a sort of Sinbad on land: wrapt up in ample corduroy dress, he bid defiance to the elements, like the adventurous pioneer, journeying whithersoever he might. He had noble qualities, disinterested principles, and enlarged views. He has the credit, at an early date, of projecting the Methodist Book Concern, that efficient engine for the diffusion of knowledge throughout the land, and second to no other establishment of a like nature among us save the Brothers Harper. No denomination has stronger reasons to be grateful to individual effort for its more enlightened condition, its increased strength, its literature, its more refined ministry, and the trophies which already adorn the brows of its scholars, than has the Methodist Church to Francis Asbury. Pilmore and Asbury were both advanced in life when I knew them. Pilmore sustained a wholesome rubicundity; Asbury exhibited traces of great care and a fixed pallor, in the service of his Master.

I will close this order of the ministry with the briefest notice I can take of Thomas Coke, the first Methodist Bishop for America consecrated by Wesley himself, in 1784, and identified with the progress of that society, both in England and in this country. He was just fifty years old when I listened to him in the summer of 1797. He was a diminutive creature, little higher than is reported to have been the pious Isaac Watts, but somewhat more portly. He had a keen visage, which his acquiline nose made the more decided, yet with his ample wig and triangular hat he bore an impressive *personnel.* His indomitable zeal and devotion were manifest to all. An Oxford scholar, a clever author, and glowing with devotional fervor, his shrill voice penetrated the remotest part of the assembly. He discoursed on God's providence, and terminated the exercises with reading the beautiful hymn of Addison, "The Lord my pasture shall prepare." So distinctly enunciatory was his manner, that he almost electrified the audience. He dealt in the pathetic, and adepts in preaching might profit by Coke. Though sixty years have elapsed since that period, I have him before me as of yesterday. Thus much of Asbury and Coke, legible characters, whole-hearted men, the primitive pioneers of methodism in this broadcast land.

I should like to have dwelt upon the character of another great apostle of the Arminian faith, Thomas F. Sargeant. He was cast much after the same physical mould as our John M. Mason. He had little gesticulation, save the occasional raising of the palms of his hands. He stood with an imposing firmness in the sacred desk. A master of intonation, his modulated yet strong and clear utterance, poured forth a flood of thought characterized by originality and profundity on christian ethics and christian faith, winning admiration and securing conviction. He was free from dogmatism, and aimed to secure his main object, to render religion the guiding rule of life. His blows were well directed to break the stubborn heart. He was a great workman in strengthening the foundation of methodism among us: but I desist from further details.

I introduce Bishop Provoost in this place, because I think our Episcopal brethren have too much overlooked the man, his learning, his liberality, and his patriotism. He had the bearing of a well-stalled Bishop, was of pleasing address, and of refined manners. He imbibed his first classical taste at King's College, and was graduated at Peter's House, Cambridge. He became skilled in the Hebrew, Greek, Latin, French, German, and Italian languages, and we have been assured he made an English poetical version of Tasso. I never listened to his sacred ministrations but once, in Old Trinity; he was then advanced in years. He was quite a proficient in Botanical knowledge, and was among the earliest in England who studied the Linnæan classification. I long ago examined his copy of "Caspar Bauhin's Historia Plantarum," whom, on a written leaf affixed to the first volume, he calls the prince of botanists, and which MS. bears date 1766. He was to the back-bone a friend to the cause of revolutionary America; and I believe it is now granted, that there was scarcely another of that religious order among us who was not a loyalist. I ought to add, that a portion of his library was given to our Society by C. D. Colden, his son-in-law, who furnished me with the MS. of his life, a few days before his death, and to which I ventured, with the approbation of Mr. Colden, to make additional facts concerning the Bishop's attainments in natural science.

Our enlightened founder, John Pintard, was personally known, during a long life, to a large majority of the citizens of this metropolis, and was universally consulted by individuals, of almost every order, for information touching this state's transactions, and the multifarious occurrences of this city, which have marked its progress since our revolutionary struggle. Persons and things, individualities and corporations, literary, biographical, ecclesiastical, and historical circumstances, municipal and legislative enactments, internal and external commerce, all these were prominent among the number; and his general accuracy as to persons and dates made him a living chronology. During a long period of his memorable life, our learned associate, Dr. Mitchill, held the same distinction in the walks of science. Pintard's life was not, however, solely retrospective: he had the capabilities of one whose vision extended far ahead. Witness his remarkable estimate of the growth of this city, in inhabitants and in extent, dating from about 1805, and comprehending a period long after his death. The fulfilment is so striking with the facts as he prognosticated, that the statistical writer cannot but marvel at the precision of his data and the fulfilment of his calculations. See, further, his earnest co-operation with De Witt Clinton and Cadwallader D. Colden, Thomas Eddy, and others, in bringing together that first mass meeting in behalf of the Erie Policy, held in the Park, when the requisites for such assumption jeoparded almost life, and cut off all political advancement. Look at his enlarged views to promote the interests of that church to which he so early and so long had claims as an exalted member, in effectually securing the noble Sherrard bequest for the Theological Seminary, and his successful application to George Lorrillard for the twenty-five thousand dollar fund for a professorship: canvass his merits for the organization of many of the libraries which now enrich this city, and the cheerful aid with which he united with the late benevolent William Wood, in furtherance of a hundred other public objects. Examine for yourselves the records of the office of the city inspector, and learn the obstacles he encountered to establish that department of the city institutions, for the registry of births and deaths. But I will no longer tire you.

Pintard's astonishing love and reverence for the past was no less remarkable. The men of the Revolution were his idols, and perhaps his longest attached and most important of this class were Willett, Jay, Fish, and Col. Trumbull. He often conversed with me of his acquaintance with Washington, Jefferson, Madison, Geo. Clinton, Rufus King, and Hamilton, but I am left to infer that with some of these his personal associations were limited. As a deputy agent under Elias Boudinot, as commissary-general for prisoners, he was fully conversant, from observation, with the horrors of the jail and the Jersey prison ship, and he never touched that subject that he did not revive reminiscences of Philip Freneau, the scenes of the old Sugar House, the hospital practice conducted by Michaelis and others on the American prisoners in the old Dutch Church, (now Post Office,) then appropriated to medical accommodation, as well as for other purposes, by the British army. It is familiarly known to my audience that our state legislature during the session of 1817–'18 passed a law, prepared by Henry Meigs, for the disinterment of the body of Montgomery in Canada for re-burial under the monument in St. Paul's Church, N. Y. Soon after the passage of the act, I waited upon Mr. Pintard on some subject connected with the Historical Society, and found his mind worried. "You seem, sir," said I, "to be embarrassed." "Somewhat so," replied he; "I have just received an Albany letter requiring specific information: they are at a loss to know where Montgomery's bones lie. I shall be able soon to give them an answer." It is almost needless to add that Pintard's directions led to the very spot where, within a few feet designated by him, the remains of the patriot were discovered.

It had long been understood that the old Chamber of Commerce had a full-length portrait, painted by Pine, of Lieut. Governor Colden. Pintard was for years in search of it: at length he had prospects of success; and ransacking the loft of the old Tontine, (recently demolished,) he discovered the prize among a parcel of old lumber. "I shall now," said he, "take measures to revive that excellent old corporation, much to be regarded for what it has done for our metropolis, and for what it is capable of doing." My friend Dr. King can scarcely forget John Pintard in his History of the Chamber of Commerce. This precious painting of Colden is now among your historical treasures.

If a careful examination be made of the earlier records of our Historical Society, it will be seen that our founder, John Pintard, filled with the idea of establishing this institution, most judiciously sought the countenance of the reverend the clergy of this metropolis. He was alive to the beneficial zeal employed by Jeremy Belknap and other divines in behalf of the Massachusetts Historical Society: he considered the clergy as among the safest guardians of literature and history, and that their recommendation of the measure would prove of signal utility. The Rev. Dr. Samuel Miller, of whom I have on several occasions spoken in laudatory terms, was at this period a prominent individual throughout the land, by the recent publication of his "Brief Retrospect," which obtained for its author the applause of both hemispheres. This able divine and courteous and exemplary character, had also announced to his friends his intention of preparing for the press a "History of the State of New York," and it was further understood that he had given much study to historical research. Dr. John M. Mason, who stood without a parallel among us as a preacher, and as a student of ecclesiastical affairs, with strong feelings for New York, was also one on whom Pintard relied for counsel. There was, moreover, so adventurous a daring in the very elements of Mason's constitution, and his personal influence was so wide among the literati, that it was inferred his countenance could not but increase the number of advocates for the plan. Innovation presented no alarm to Dr. Mason; progress was his motto. He had heard much of revolutionary times from the lips of his friend Hamilton. His father's patriotism circulated in his veins: he knew the uncertainties of historical data, and that the nation's history, as well as that of the State's, was yet to be written. This heroic scholar and divine, whom I never think of without admiration of the vastness of intellectual power which God in his wisdom vouchsafes to certain mortals, was prominently acknowledged as the chieftain of the ecclesiastical brotherhood of those days. He contemplated, moreover, a life of his friend Hamilton, and doubtless was often absorbed in the consideration of American history. The paramount obligations of his pastoral and scholastic duties, and their imperative urgency, must unquestionably be assigned as reasons for his non-performance. As a reader he was unrivalled; as an orator in the sacred desk, his disciplined intellect shed its radiance over all he uttered. Rich in a knowledge of mankind, and of the ethics of nations, the ample treasures of ancient and modern learning were summoned at command, with a practical influence at which doubt fled, and sophistry and indifference stood abashed. He was bold in his animadversions on public events, and lashed the vices of the times with unsparing severity. There was no equivocation in his nature, either in sentiment or in manner. His address to his people, on resigning his pastoral charge of the Cedar Street Church, is, perhaps, his greatest oratorical effort. His Plea for Sacramental Communion evinced a toleration worthy of apostolic Christianity: his address on the formation of the American Bible Society, prepared within a few hours for the great occasion, by its masculine vigor crushed opposition even in high quarters, and led captive the convention. "We have not a man among us," said Olinthus Gregory, of the British Society, "who can cope with your Mason. All have wondered at the sublimity and earnestness of his address." In his conversation Dr. Mason was an intellectual gladiator, while his commanding person and massive front added force to his argument. He knew the ductility of words, and generally chose the strongest for strongest thoughts. He had a nomenclature which he often strikingly used. In reference to an individual whose support to a certain measure was about to be solicited, "Put no confidence in him," said the doctor, "he's a lump of negation." In speaking of the calamitous state of the wicked and the needy in times of pestilence, he broke forth in this language:—"To be poor in this world, and to be damned in the next, is to be miserable indeed." He had a deep hatred of the old-fashioned pulpit, which he called an ecclesiastical tub, and said it cramped both mind and body. With

Whitfield, he wished the mountain for a pulpit, and the heavens for a sounding-board. His example in introducing the platform in its stead has proved so effective, that he may claim the merit of having led to an innovation which has already become almost universal among us. As Dr. Mason is historical, and a portion of our Society's treasure, I could not be more brief concerning him. If ever mortal possessed decision of character, that mortal was John M. Mason.

Pintard, thus aided by the coöperation of so many and worthy individuals in professional life, determined to prosecute his design with vigor. He had doubtless submitted his plan to his most reliable friend De Witt Clinton, at an early day of its inception, and it is most probable that by their concurrence Judge Egbert Benson was selected as the most judicious choice for first President. This venerable man had long been an actor in some of the most trying scenes of his country's legislative history, and was himself the subject of history. His antecedents were all favorable to his being selected: of Dutch parentage, a native of the city of New York, and a distinguished classical scholar of King's College, from which he was graduated in 1765. He was one of the Committee of Safety: deeply read in legal matters, and as a proficient in the science of pleading, he had long been known as holding a high rank in jurisprudence. By an ordinance of the Convention of 1777, he was appointed first Attorney-General of the State—he was also a member of the first legislature of 1777. Perhaps it may be new to some of my hearers to learn, that he was also one of the three Commissioners appointed by the United States to assist with other Commissioners that might be chosen by Sir Guy Carleton, to superintend the embarkation of the tories for Nova Scotia. The letter to Carleton of their appointment signed by Judge Egbert Benson, William Smith, and Daniel Parker, bears date New York, June 17, 1783. I am indebted to our faithful historian, Mr. Lossing, for this curious fact.

In 1789 Mr. Benson was elected one of the six Representatives of New York to the first Congress, in which body he continued four years. In his Congressional career, he was often associated in measures with Rufus King, Fisher Ames, Oliver Ellsworth, and others of the same illustrious order of men. Nor did his official public services end here. In 1794 he was appointed a Judge of the Supreme Court of New York, where he remained several years. He was a Regent of the University from 1789 to 1802. He was a most intimate and reliable friend of that stern and inflexible patriot, Gov. John Jay. He lived the admiration of all good men to the very advanced age of 87 years, blessed with strength of body and soundness of mind, and died at Jamaica, on Long Island, in 1833, confident in the triumphs of a Christian life.

The patriotism of Judge Benson, his devotion to his country in its most trying vicissitudes, his political and moral integrity, were never questioned. His kindliness of feeling, and his social and unassuming demeanor, struck every beholder. Such was Egbert Benson, the individual earliest and wisely pointed out as our first President.

My acquaintance with Judge Benson did not commence until near the close of his official tenure in this Society. He presided at the first great festival we held in 1809, at the delivery of Dr. Miller's Discourse, on the 4th of September, 1809, designed to commemorate the discovery of New York, being the completion of the second century since that event. I have, on a former occasion, given an account of that celebration. Judge Benson was anecdotical in an eminent degree: his iron memory often gave proofs of its tenacity. His reminiscences of his native city are often evinced in his curious Record of New York in the olden times. From him I learned that our noble faculty of physic had, in those earlier days, their disputations, theoretical and practical, as we have witnessed them in our own times. Strong opposition was met in those days to the adoption of inoculation for the small-pox, as pursued by Dr. Beekman Van Beuren, in the old Alms House, prior to 1770. Old McGrath, a violent Scotchman, who came among us about 1743, and who is immortalized by Smollett, had the honor of introducing the free use of cold bathing and cold lavations in fever. He doubtless had drawn his notions from Sir John Floyer, but probably had never conceived a single principle enforced by Currie. McGrath's whole life was a perpetual turmoil. Dr. Henry Mott, who died in 1840, aged 83 years, and the father of the illustrious surgeon Dr. Valentine Mott, was among the prominent practitioners who adopted the mercurial practice, with Ogden and Muirson, of Long Island, not without much opposition. But the most serious rencontre in our medical annals, according to the Judge, was that which took place with Dr. Pierre Michaux, a French refugee, who settled in New York about 1791, who published an English tract on a surgical subject, with a Latin title-page. The pamphlet was too insignificant to prove an advantageous advertisement to the penniless author, but Dr. Wright Post, of most distinguished renown in our records of surgery, feeling annoyed by its appearance, solicited his intimate friend, the acrimonious Dunlap, the dramatic writer, to write a caricature of the work and the author. The request was promptly complied with, and at the old John Street Theatre a ludicrous after-piece was got up, illustrative of a surgical case, *Fractura Minimi Digiti*, with a meeting of doctors in solemn consultation upon the catastrophy. Michaux repaired to the theatre, took his seat among the spectators, and found the representation of his person, his dress, his manner, and his speech, so fairly a veri-resemblance, that he was almost ready to admit an alibi, and alternately thought himself now among the audience—now among the performers. The humiliated Michaux sought redress by an assault upon Dunlap, as, on the ensuing Sabbath, he was coming out from worship in the Brick Church. The violent castigation Dunlap received at the church portal, suspended his public devotional duties for at least a month. Michaux, now the object of popular ridicule, retired to Staten Island, where after a while his life was closed, oppressed with penury, and mortification of mind. I have thus (by way of parenthesis) introduced some things touching the doctors of years past. I crave your clemency for the interruption. I am so constituted, that I cannot avoid a notice of our departed medical men whenever I address New Yorkers on the subject of their city. I must plead, moreover, that these medical anecdotes are connected with the materials I derived from Judge Benson himself. They in part illustrate his minute recognition of events and his tenacious recollection.

So intimately connected with history is the record of juridical proceedings, and the actors thereof, the actual founders of statutory measures, especially in our popular form of government, that state events necessarily receive their distinctive features from the members of the bar. In short, is not the statute book the most faithful history of a people? Mr. Pintard, with the largest views to success, earnestly sought the coöperation of that enlightened and important profession. The laws of a nation, said he, are pre-eminently historical in their nature, and fall within our scope. I am justified in the assertion, from personal knowledge, that no class of our citizens embarked with greater zeal in strengthening the interests of this Association than did the members of that faculty. If you search the minutes of our proceedings, you will find they constitute a large portion of our early friends, and that, too, at a period when the idea of rearing this establishment was pronounced preposterous, by many even of the well informed.

I shall glance at a few of these worthies among our earliest, our strongest, and most devoted supporters. Anthony Bleecker, who deserves an ample memoir, was a native of the city of New York; he was born in October, 1770, and died in March, 1827. He was a graduate of Columbia College, reared to the profession of the law, and was a gentleman of classical acquisitions, and refined belles-lettres taste. As a member of the Drone Club, a social and literary circle, which had at that time an existence of some years among us, and which included among its members Kent, Johnson, Dunlap, Edward and Samuel Miller, and Charles Brockden Brown, he proved an efficient associate in our ranks. He was for many years a prolific contributor to the periodical press, in elegant literature, and wrote for the Drone in prose and verse. Well stored in historical and topographical matters, not a small portion of our library, which contains our early literature, was due to his inquisitive spirit. His sympathies were ever alive to acts of disinterested benevolence, and as proof we may state that from the crude notes, journals, and log-books which Capt. James Riley furnished, Bleecker drew up gratuitously that popular "Narrative of the Brig Commerce," which obtained so wide a circulation both in this country and abroad. He was almost unceasingly engaged in American records of a literary nature, and was just such a scholar for a contributor as the English "Notes and Queries" would have solicited for their work. He wrote to Bisset, the English writer of the reign of George III., to correct the error which he had promulgated, that Henry Cruger, the colleague of Burke, had circumscribed his speech to the enunciation of three words, "I say ditto;" and which Bisset finally cancelled in subsequent reprints. The productions of Mr. Bleecker's pen were such as to make his friends regret that he did not elaborate a work on some weighty subject. He died a Christian death, in 1827, aged 59 years. His habits, his morals, his weight of character, may be inferred from the mention of his associates, Irving, Paulding, Verplanck, and Brevoort. The bar passed sympathizing resolutions on his demise, and John Pintard lost a wise counsellor. The portrait of Mr. Bleecker in the N. Y. Society Library, is a lifelike work of art.

William Johnson is of too recent death not to be held in fresh remembrance by many now present. He was a native of Connecticut; he settled early in New York, and entered upon the profession of the law, and was engaged from 1806 to 1823 as Reporter of the Supreme Court of New York, and from 1814 to 1823, of the Court of Chancery. He died in 1848, when he had passed his 80th year. He is recorded in the original act of your incorporation. He for many years had a watchful eye over the interests of the Society. It is beyond my province to speak of the value of his labors. He was of a calm and dignified bearing, and of the strictest integrity. As he was the authorized reporter of the legal decisions of the State at a period when her juridical science was expounded by her greatest masters, Kent, Spencer, Van Nest, Thompson, &c., and was at its highest renown and of corresponding authority throughout the Union, his numerous volumes are pronounced the most valuable we possess in the department of the law. He was liberal in his donations of that part of our library devoted to jurisprudence. His most interesting historical contributions to the library were those of the newspaper press:—the New York Daily Advertiser from its commencement, an uninterrupted series, until near its close, and the New York Evening Post from its beginning in 1801, and for many consecutive years, may be cited as proofs in point.

With an earnestness surpassed by none of our earlier fraternity, the late Peter A. Jay espoused the cause of this institution, and contributed largely to its library. His benefactions embraced much of that curious and most valuable material you find classed with your rare list of newspapers, printed long before our Revolutionary contest. I apprehend he must have been thus enabled through the liberality of his illustrious father, Governor Jay. Peter A. Jay was most solicitous in all his doings touching the Society, that the association should restrict itself to its specified designation. Every thing relative to its historical transactions he would cherish, for he deemed New York the theatre on which the great events of the period of our colonization and of the war of independence transpired. It is in no wise remarkable that the library is so rich in newspaper and other periodical journals. "A file of American newspapers," said Mr. Jay, "is of far more value to our design, than all the Byzantine historians." You may well boast of the vast accumulation of that species of recorded knowledge within your walls.

So far as I can recollect, our most efficient members, as Johnson, Jay, Pintard, M'Kesson, Clinton, Morris, and a host of others, have borne testimony to the high importance of preserving those too generally evanescent documents. They are the great source from which we are to derive our knowledge of the form and pressure of the times. No one was more emphatic in the declaration of this opinion than Gouverneur Morris.

John M'Kesson, a nephew of the M'Kesson who was Secretary of the N. Y. Convention, an original member, was a large contributor to our Legislative documents; not the least in value of which were the Journals of the Provincial Congress and Convention, together with the proceedings of the Committee of Safety from May, 1775, to the adoption of the State Constitution at the close of the Northern campaign in 1777. "They include," says our distinguished associate, Mr. Folsom, "the period of the invasion of the territory of the State by the British army under General Burgoyne."

The minutes of our first meeting notice the attendance of Samuel Bayard, jun. He was connected by marriage with the family of our founder, Pintard, and they were most intimate friends. He was a gentleman of the old school, a scholar, a jurist, a trustee of Princeton College, a public-spirited man, and a hearty cooperator in establishing this association. Widely acquainted with historical occurrences, and, if I err not, on terms of personal communication with many of the active men of the Revolution, including Governor Livingston, of New Jersey, through Mr. Bayard's agency, and John Pintard, we obtained the Independent Reflector, the Watch Tower of 1754, the American Whig, &c., records indispensable to a right understanding of the controversy of the American Episcopate, and the contentions which sprung out of the charter of King's College. Livingston's life is full of occurrences: he was a voluminous writer on the side of liberty, when his country most needed such advocates: his patriotism was of the most intrepid order, and he commanded the approbation of Washington. Theodore Sedgwick, not long since, has given us his valuable biography, and the Duyckincks in the "Cyclopædia of American Literature," a legacy of precious value, for the consultation of writers on the progress of knowledge in the New World, have treated his character and his labors with ability and impartiality. Some forty years ago, I saw the prospectus for the publication of Governor Livingston's works, in several volumes, at the office of the Messrs. Collins. Had the plan been executed, the arm of the patriot would have been nerved with increased strength in behalf of religious toleration and the rights of man, by the noble defence of this bold explorer into the domain of popular freedom. But, alas! the materials for the contemplated work, in print and in manuscript, were suffered to lie in neglect in a printing loft, until time and the rats had destroyed them too far for typographical purposes. I was told that his son, Brockholst Livingston, the renowned United States judge, had the matter in charge, and I have presumed that the remembrance of his father's literary labors was obliterated from his memory, through the weightier responsibilities of juridical business. I believe we are obligated to Samuel Bayard principally for that remarkable series of MSS., the Journals of the House of Commons during the Protectorate of Cromwell, which fill so conspicuous a niche in your library. Mr. Bayard, I apprehend, obtained them through Governor Livingston, or, perhaps, I would be more accurate, were I to say, that they were once in the possession of the Governor. I remember bringing over from Paulus Hook, now Jersey City, some of the volumes.

We possessed liberal benefactors in our earlier movements for a library, in Samuel M. Hopkins, Cadwallader D. Colden, and Gulian C. Verplanck. This last named gentleman, who is recorded as an early member, and whom, thanks to a beneficent Providence, we still hail among the living celebrities of the Republic, both in letters and in humanity, stored with varied knowledge, and actuated by true Knickerbocker feelings, deemed the library department of enduring importance, and with a comprehensive view affirmed, that it was the bounden duty of the Society to collect every book, pamphlet, chart, map, or newspaper that threw light on the progress of the State, its cities, towns, or on the history of its literature; thus carrying out the plan unfolded in the Society's address to the public at their first organization. That we profit by more than his advice, may be seen in his historical discourse on the early European friends of America, and the tribute he pays to the character of our forefathers, the Dutch and the Huguenots.

From the studies and accomplishments of the well-instructed physician, from the wide range of knowledge, physical and mental, that falls within his observation; from the fact that every department of Nature must be explored, the better to discipline him properly to exercise his art; the inference may be readily drawn that the faculty of medicine would scarcely prove indifferent to the creation of an institution fraught with such incentives to intellectual culture, as are necessarily embraced within the range and intentions of our Historical Society. Moreover, I incline to the belief, that veneration for our predecessors is somewhat a characteristic of the cultivators of medical philosophy: the past is not to be overlooked, and the means for its preservation is in itself an intellectual advancement. The concurrence of the leading medical men of that early day was proved by the fellowship of Hosack, Bruce, Mitchill, Miller, Williamson, and, shortly after, by N. Romayne, and others of renown. These distinguished characters need no commendation of ours at this time. Your secretary has made records of their services, and it has so chanced, that, from personal intimacy, I have long ago been enabled to present humble memorials in different places, of their professional influence and deeds. They were men of expansive views, nor were the elements of practical utility idle in their hands. Of my preceptor and friend, David Hosack, let it be sufficient to remark that, distinguished beyond all his competitors in the healing art, for a long series of years, he was acknowledged, by every hearer, to have been the most eloquent and impressive teacher of scientific medicine and clinical practice this country has produced. He was, indeed, a great instructor ; his descriptive powers and his diagnosis were the admiration of all ; his efficiency in rearing, to a state of high consideration, the College of Physicians and Surgeons, while he held the responsible office of professor, is known throughout the Republic ; his early movements to establish a medical library in the New York Hospital ; his coöperation with the numerous charities which glorify the metropolis ; his adventurous outlay for the establishment of a State Botanical Garden ; his hygienic suggestions the better to improve the medical police of New York ; his primary formation of a mineralogical cabinet ; his copious writings on fever, quarantines, and foreign pestilence, in which he was the strenuous and almost the sole advocate for years, of doctrines now verified by popular demonstration ; these, and a thousand other circumstances, secured to him a weight of character that was almost universally felt throughout the metropolis. It was not unfrequently remarked by our citizens, that Clinton, Hosack, and Hobart were the tripod on which our city stood. The lofty aspirations of Hosack were further evinced by his whole career as a citizen. Surrounded by his large and costly library, his house was the resort of the learned and enlightened from every part of the world. No traveller from abroad rested satisfied without a personal interview with him ; and, at his evening soirées, the literati, the philosopher, and the statesman, the skilful in natural science, and the explorer of new regions; the archæologist and the theologue met together, participators in the recreation of familiar intercourse. Your printed volumes contain all, I believe, he ever prepared for you as your President. His life was a triumph in services rendered and in honors received; his death was a loss to New York, the city of his birth; his remains were followed to the grave by the eminent of every profession, and by the humble in life whom his art had relieved. Hosack was a man of profuse expenditure; he regarded money only for what it might command. Had he possessed the wealth of John Jacob Astor, he might have died poor.

Early at the commencement of your patriotic undertaking was recorded Archibald Bruce as a member. We had, at that time, more than one Bruce in the faculty among us. He of the Historical Society was the physician and mineralogist. He was born in New York in 1771, was graduated at Columbia College, studied medicine with Hosack, and, in 1800, received the doctorate at the Edinburgh University. While in Scotland, he acquired a knowledge of the Wernerian theory under Jameson, and subsequently became a correspondent of the Abbé Haüy, the founder of Crystallography. He collected a large cabinet of minerals while travelling about in Europe, projected the "American Journal of Mineralogy" in 1810, the first periodical of that science in the United States, and was created Mineralogical Professor by the regents of the University, at the organization of the College of Physicians and Surgeons. He had a cultivated taste for the Fine Arts, and contributed to our Library.

He died in 1818. His reputation rests with his discovery, at Hoboken, of the Hydrate of Magnesia. In "Silliman's Journal" there is a biography of him.

The universal praise which Dr. Mitchill enjoyed in almost every part of the globe where science is cultivated, during a long life, is demonstrative that his merits were of a high order. A discourse might be delivered on the variety and extent of his services in the cause of learning and humanity; and as his biography is already before the public in the "National Portrait Gallery," and we are promised that by Dr. Akerly, I have little to say at this time but what may be strictly associated with our Institution. His character had many peculiarities: his knowledge was diversified and most extensive, if not always profound. Like most of our sex, he was married; but, as Old Fuller would say, the only issues of his body were the products of his brain. He advanced the scientific reputation of New York by his early promulgation of the Lavoisierian system of chemistry, when first appointed professor in Columbia College: his first scientific paper was an essay on Evaporation: his mineralogical survey of New York, in 1797, gave Volney many hints: his analysis of the Saratoga waters enhanced the importance of those mineral springs. His ingenious theory of septic acid gave impulse to Sir Humphry Davy's vast discoveries: his doctrines on pestilence awakened inquiry from every class of observers throughout the Union: his expositions of a theory of the earth and solar system, captivated minds of the highest qualities. His correspondence with Priestley is an example of the delicious manner in which argument can be conducted in philosophical discussion: his elaborate account of the fishes of our waters invoked the plaudits of Cuvier. His reflections on Somnium evince psychological views of original combination. His numerous papers on natural history enriched the annals of the Lyceum, of which he was long president. His researches on the ethnological characteristics of the red man of America, betrayed the benevolence of his nature and his generous spirit: his fanciful article for a new and more appropriate geographical designation for the United States, was at one period a topic which enlisted a voluminous correspondence, now printed in your Proceedings. He increased our knowledge of the vegetable materia medica of the United States. He wrote largely to Percival on noxious agents. He cheered Fulton when dejected; encouraged Livingston in appropriation; awakened new zeal in Wilson the ornithologist, when the Governor, Tompkins, had nigh paralyzed him by his frigid and unfeeling reception; and, with Pintard and Colden, was a zealous promoter of that system of internal improvement which has stamped immortality on the name of Clinton. He coöperated with Jonathan Williams in furtherance of the Military Academy at West Point, and for a long series of years was an important professor of useful knowledge in Columbia College and in the College of Physicians and Surgeons. His letter to Tilloch, of London, on the progress of his mind in the investigation of septic acid, is curious as a physiological document. The leading papers from his pen are to be found in the New York Medical Repository; yet he wrote in the American Medical and Philosophical Register, the New York Medical and Physical Journal, the American Mineralogical Journal, and supplied several other periodicals, both abroad and at home, with the results of his cogitations. He was one of the commissioners appointed by the general government for the construction of a new naval force to be propelled by steam, the steamer Fulton the First. While he was a member of the United States Senate, he was unwearied in effecting the adoption of improved quarantine laws; and, among his other acts, strenuous to lessen the duties on the importation of rags, in order to render the manufacture of paper cheaper, to aid the diffusion of knowledge by printing.

There was a rare union in Dr. Mitchill of a mind of vast and multifarious knowledge and of poetic imagery. Even in his "Epistles to his Lady Love," the excellent lady who became his endeared wife, he gave utterance of his emotions in tuneful numbers, and likened his condition unto that of the dove, with trepidation seeking safety in the ark. Ancient and modern languages were unlocked to him, and a wide range in physical science, the pabulum of his intellectual repast. An essay on composts, a tractate on the deaf and dumb, verses to Septon or to the Indian tribes, might be eliminated from his mental alembic within the compass of a few hours. He was now engaged with the anatomy of the egg, and now deciphering a Babylonian brick; now involved in the nature of meteoric stones, now on the different species of brassica; now on the evaporization of fresh water, now on that of salt; now offering suggestions to Garnet, of New Jersey, the correspondent of Mark Akenside, on the angle of the windmill, and now concurring with Micheaux on the beauty of the black walnut as ornamental for parlor furniture. In the morning he might be found composing songs for the nursery, at noon dietetically experimenting and writing on fishes, or unfolding a new theory on terrene formations, and at evening addressing his fair readers on the healthy influences of the alkalis, and the depurative virtues of whitewashing. At his country retreat at Plandome he might find full employment in translating, for his mental diversion, Lancisi on the fens and marshes of Rome, or in rendering into English poetry the piscatory eclogues of Sannazarius. Yesterday, in workmanlike dress, he might have been engaged, with his friend Elihu H. Smith, on the natural history of the American elk, or perplexed as to the alimentary nature of tadpoles, on which, according to Noah Webster, the people of Vermont almost fattened during a season of scarcity; to-day, attired in the costume of a native of the Feejee Islands, (for presents were sent him from all quarters of the globe,) he was better accoutred for illustration, and for the reception, at his house, of a meeting of his philosophical acquaintance; while to-morrow, in the scholastic robes of an LL. D., he would grace the exercises of a college commencement.

I never encountered one of more wonderful memory: when quite a young man he would return from church service, and write out the sermon nearly verbatim. There was little display in his habits or manners. His means of enjoyment corresponded with his desires, and his Franklinean principles enabled him to rise superior to want. With all his official honors and scientific testimonials, foreign or native, he was ever accessible to everybody; the counsellor of the young, the dictionary of the learned. To the interrogatory, why he did not, after so many years of labor, revisit abroad the scenes of his earlier days for recreation, his reply was brief:—"I know Great Britain from the Grampian Hills to the chalky Cliffs of Dover: there is no need of my going to Europe, Europe now comes to me." But I must desist. The Historical Society of New York will long cherish his memory for the distinction he shed over our institution, his unassuming manners, his kind nature, and the aid he was ever ready to give to all who needed his counsel. He furnished an eulogium on our deceased member the great jurist, Thomas Addis Emmet, also on Samuel Bard; his discourse on the Botany of North and South America, is printed by the society in their Collections. Mitchill has not unjustly been pronounced the Nestor of American science.

The claims of Edward Miller to your remembrance are associated with those of his brother Samuel. Edward Miller, learned and accomplished as a scholar, generous and humane as a physician, urbane and refined as a gentleman, was of that order of intellect that could at once see the relationship which such a society as this holds with philosophy, and the record of those occurrences on which philosophy is founded. That he aided his reverend brother in that portion of the "Brief Retrospect" which treats of science in general, and of medicine in particular, was often admitted by the gifted divine. I have in strong recollection the enthusiastic terms in which Dr. Edward Miller spoke of our organization at the memorable anniversary in 1809; and all versed in our medical annals can give none other than approbation of his professional writings, though they may maintain widely different opinions from some inculcated by other observers. He survived the commencement of the society but a few years, dying in March, 1812. I accompanied him, in consultation, in the last professional visit he made, in a case of pneumonia, a few weeks before his death. In the sick room he was a cordial for affliction. His biography was written by his brother, and a memoir of his life may be found in the American Medical and Philosophical Register, vol. third.

I will close the record of our friends belonging to the medical faculty, with a brief notice of two other members, Hugh Williamson and Nicholas Romayne; the former by birth a Pennsylvanian, born in 1735, the latter a native, born in the city of New York 1756. After the acquisition of sound preliminary knowledge, Williamson was graduated M.D. at the University of Utrecht, Holland. He practised physic but a short time in Philadelphia, on account of delicate health. In 1769 he was appointed chairman of a committee consisting of Rittenhouse, Ewing, Smith, the provost, and Charles Thompson, afterwards secretary to Congress, all mathematicians and astronomers, to observe the transit of Venus in 1769. He published an Essay on Comets, afterwards enlarged, and printed in the Transactions of the Literary and Philosophical Society of New York. By appointment with Dr. Ewing, he made a tour in Great Britain in 1773, for the benefit of a literary institution. He wrote on the Gmynotius electricus, and upon his return to North Carolina was an active agent in the promotion of inoculation, and finally received a commission as head of the medical staff of the American army of that State. In 1782 he took his seat as a representative of Edenton in the House of Commons of North Carolina. In 1786 he was one of the few members who were sent to Annapolis on the amendment of the constitution, and in 1789 we find him in New York, and in the first Congress, when the constitution was carried into effect. He wrote an octavo volume on the climate of America. In 1812 appeared his History of North Carolina. He was the author of several papers on medical and philosophical subjects, and on the canal policy of the state, printed in the American Medical and Philosophical Register. He was among the first of our citizens who entertained correct views on the practicability of the union of the waters of the Hudson and Lake Erie. He penned the first summons for the formation of the Literary and Philosophical Society of New York. He died in 1819, at the advanced age of 83 years.

The career of Williamson is well known from the ample Biography of his friend and physician, Dr. Hosack. He was justly esteemed for his talents, his virtues, and his public services. Hosack affirmed on the testimony of Bishop White, John Adams, President of the United States, Gen. Reed, and John Williamson, that Hugh Williamson was the individual who, by an ingenious device, obtained the famous Hutchinson and Oliver letters from the British foreign office for Franklin, and I can add that John Williamson, the brother of the doctor, communicated to me his concurrence in the same testimony. This curious relation is however rejected as not well founded, by our eminent historians, Sparks and Bancroft.

Williamson was a peculiarity in appearance, in manners, and in address. Tall and slender in person, with an erect gait, he perambulated the streets with the air of a man of consideration; his long arms and his longer cane preceding him at commanding distance, and seemingly guided by his conspicuous nose, while his ample white locks gave tokens of years and wisdom. Activity of mind and body blessed him to the last of his long life. His speech was brief, sententious, and emphatic. He was often aphoristic, always pertinacious in opinion. There was rarely an appeal from his decision—he was generally so well fortified. He had great reverence for the past, was anecdotical in our revolutionary matters, and cherished with almost reverential regard the series of cocked hats which he had worn at different times, during the eight years' crisis of his country. His History of North Carolina has encountered the disapprobation of many, and is deemed defective and erroneous, yet he was a devoted disciple of truth. No flattery, no compliment would ever reach his ear. Witness his curt correspondence with the Italian artist, Carrachi: look at his testimony in the case of Alexander Whisteloe. To a solicitation for pecuniary aid in behalf of an individual whose moral character he somewhat doubted, when told that a reform had taken place: "Not so," replied the doctor, "he has not left the stage,—the stage has left him." His punctuality in engagements was marvellous; no hour, no wind or weather, ever occasioned a disappointment on the part of the old man, now over eighty years of age; and in his own business transactions, of which from various incomes he derived his ample support, one might apprehend the requirement of much time, he let not the setting sun close upon him without their entire adjustment. He died, if I remember rightly, about the hour of 4 o'clock of the afternoon, while in a carriage excursion to the country, from excessive solar heat, in June;

yet it was found that his multifarious accounts and correspondence had all been adjusted, up to the hour of two on that same day.

Some of my most gratifying hours in early life were passed with this venerable man: it was instructive to enjoy the conversation of one who had enriched the pages of the Royal Society; who had experimented with John Hunter, and Franklin, and Ingenhouze in London, and had enjoyed the soirées of Sir John Pringle; who narrated occurrences in which he bore a part when Franklin was Postmaster, and in those of subsequent critical times; one, who, if you asked him the size of the button on Washington's coat, might tell you who had been his tailor. A more strictly correct man, in all fiscal matters, could not be pointed out, whether in bonds and mortgages, or in the payment of the postage of a letter. I will give an illustration. He had been appointed in Colonial times to obtain funds for the Seminary at Baskenridge, N. J.: he set out on his eastern tour, provided with an extra pair of gloves, for which he paid 7*s.* and 6*d.*: on his return he revisited the store in Newark, where he had made the purchase, had the soiled gloves vamped anew, and parted with them for 6*s.* In his items of expenditure, he reports 1*s.* and 6*d.* for the use of gloves, investing the 6*s.* with the collection fund. Such was Hugh Williamson, whose breastplate was honesty, the brightest in the Christian armory. If I mistake not, I think I once saw him smile at the trick of a jockey. Dr. Thacher, the author of the "Military Journal," told me he had listened to him when he was in the ministry, in a sermon preached at Plymouth; but his oratory was grotesque, and Rufus King the Senator, who noticed him in our first Congress, said his elocution provoked laughter. Yet he spoke to the point. Take him altogether, he was admirably fitted for the times, and conscientiously performed many deeds of excellence for the period in which he lived. Deference was paid to him by every class of citizens. He holds a higher regard in my estimation, than a score of dukes and duchesses, for he signed the Constitution of the United States. His Anniversary Discourse for 1810, you have secured in your publications. The portrait of Dr. Williamson by Col. Trumbull, is true to the life and eminently suggestive.

A monograph on Romayne would not be too much. He entered the Historical Society some years after its formation. He is associated with innumerable occurrences in New York, his native city, and was born in 1756. Of his antecedents little is satisfactorily known. His early instruction was received from Peter Wilson, the linguist, at his school at Hackensack. At the commencement of the war of the Revolution he repaired to Edinburgh, where he pre-eminently distinguished himself by his wide range of studies, his latinity and his medical knowledge. His inaugural for the doctorate, prepared unassisted, was a dissertation De Generatione Puris, in which he seems to have first promulgated the leading doctrines received on that vexed subject. He now visited London, Paris, and Leyden, for further knowledge, and returning to his native land, settled first in Philadelphia, and shortly after in New York. He had a fair chance of becoming a practitioner of extensive employment. His erudition justified him in assuming the office of teacher, and he lectured with success on several branches of physic. He was pronounced an extraordinary man. Anatomy, chemistry, botany, and the practice of medicine, were assumed by him. His most eminent associates, Bayley, Kissam, Moore, Treat, and Tillary, echoed his praises. He spoke with fluency the French and Latin tongues, and the low Dutch.

When the provincial government of King's College was changed after 1783, he was nominated one of the Trustees. The Board of the College, now Columbia, determined upon reviving a new faculty of medicine, but from causes too numerous to relate, Dr. Romayne was not chosen to an appointment. In 1791, an act was passed, authorizing the Regents of the University to organize a medical faculty, which, however, did not go into operation until January, 1807, when Dr. Romayne was appointed President of the College of Physicians and Surgeons under their authority. He gave lectures on Anatomy and on the Institutes. I was present at his opening address to the students at the ensuing November. It was an elegant and elaborate performance in science and on the ethnology of the red man of America. He was a pleasing speaker; his discourse justified all that had been previously expressed concerning his varied knowledge and his classical taste. He would rise in his place and deliver a lecture on the aphorisms of Hippocrates, unfold the structure of the brain, expound the philosophy of paludal diseases, or discourse on the plant which Clusius cherished. He was indeed clever in every acceptation of the word. I find since that period, by an examination of his copy of the Conspectus Medicinæ of Gregory, and his MS. notes, that his Lectures on the Institutions were drawn chiefly from Gregory's work. Yet was he an original observer and an intrepid thinker. He died suddenly, after great exposure to heat, in June, 1817.

It rarely occurs to any individual to enjoy a larger renown among his fellows, than did Dr. Romayne during the time he filled the station of President of the College. Yet he was not content with this condition of affairs, and was constantly studying new things, until ejected from his high office by the Regents of the University, the venerable Samuel Bard being chosen as his successor.

His penury in early life had taught Romayne the strictest economy. At Edinburgh his wardrobe was so slender, that it often reminded me of the verses of an old ballad:—

"The man who has only one shirt,
Whenever it's washed for his side,
The offence is surely not his
If he lies in his bed till it's dried."

Such, literally, was the case with the student Romayne, and still he bore himself with becoming respectability, and left the University one of the most accomplished of her sons in general knowledge and professional science. He did well enough during his two years in Philadelphia as a practitioner; an equally favorable turn in business followed him in New York, in which place he settled as the British troops left the city. The spirit of adventure, however, seized him: he embarked in the scheme of Blount's conspiracy, was seized by the constituted authorities, and Pintard saw him conveyed to prison. In what manner his troubles were removed I am unable to state. I have heard of no special disclosures that he made. He was too long-headed for self-accusation, and however bellicose by nature, preferred his customary cautious habit. Romayne had learned the proverb of the old Hebrews:—"One word is worth a shekel—silence is worth two." But awhile after he revisited Europe, became a licentiate of the Royal College of Edinburgh, returned to his native city, and was chosen President of the College, an institution of only two years later date than your own, and which, amidst great vicissitudes and an anomalous government, has enriched with meritorious disciples the noble art of healing, and diffused untold blessings throughout the land.

Romayne was of huge bulk, of regular proportion, and of an agreeable and intelligent expression of countenance, with a gray eye of deep penetration. It was almost a phenomenon to witness the light, gracious, and facile step of a man surpassing some three hundred pounds in weight, and at all times assiduous in civic pursuits and closet studies. He was unwearied in toil, and of mighty energy. He was goaded by a strong ambition to excel in whatever he undertook, and he generally secured the object of his desire, at least professionally. He was temperate in all his drinks, but his gastric powers were of inordinate capabilities. I should incur your displeasure were I to record the material of a single meal: he sat down with right good earnest and exclusive devotion at his repast. His auricular power seemed now suspended. Dr. Mitchill long ago had said that the stomach had no ears. In charity I have conjectured that he must have labored under a species of bulimia, which pathologists affirm will often pervert the moral faculties. His kind friend, the late Reverend Dr. M'Leod, tells us, that though many of his acts were crooked, yet that Romayne died in the consolations of the Christian religion. He was generous to the young, and ready with many resources to advance the student. He made a great study of man; he was dexterous with legislative bodies, and at one period of his career was vested with almost all the honors the medical profession among us can bestow. Some of the older medical writers, whose works were found in the residue of the library of the late Dr. Peter Middleton, as well as others of the late Dr. Romayne, were deposited in your library; but of late years, I am sorry to say, I have not recognized them.

I shall now take leave of the departed doctors, while memory cannot forget their living excellence, and cast a glance at some few circumstances, which, more or less immediate or remote, had an influence in fostering those associations which finally accelerated public opinion, and led to the establishment of the Historical Society at the fortunate epoch at which it was organized.

The extraordinary occurrences of the American Revolution, which had left their impress on the minds of most of the patriots who had survived that mighty event, the peace of 1783, which closed the great drama, and now presented the country impoverished and in debt, its resources exhausted, its people rich in a knowledge of their rights, yet poor indeed in fiscal power, were circumstances calculated to awaken a personal interest, more or less deep, in every bosom, and to excite inquiry, with a curious scrutiny, what history would unfold of the marvellous trials through which the people had passed, and what historian would write the faithful record of their sufferings and their deeds.

This city, which had been the occupancy of their

enemies during that long struggle, though now freed of the British army, still retained a vast number of the Tory party, who, while they were ready to be the participators of the benefits of that freedom which sprung out of the Revolution, were known to be disaffected by the mortifications of defeat, under which they still writhed, and whose principal relief was found in yielding the listening ear to any narrative that might asperse the purity of American devotion in the patriotic cause of freedom. Thus surrounded, the natives, the true Whigs, the rebel phalanx, so to speak, were often circumscribed in thought and in utterance. To recount the specifications of the wrongs which they had endured, as cited in the immortal Declaration of Independence, was deemed, by the defeated and disaffected, cruel and unwise, so hard was it to root out the doctrines of colonial devotion. Here and there measures were in agitation, and suggestions hinted, the object of which was to prevent the public reading of the Declaration on the 4th of July; and even so late as July, 1804, a turmoil arose, upon the occasion of the expressed sentiments of the orator of the day, John W. Mulligan, Esq., now, I believe, the oldest living graduate of Columbia College.

It was in vain that appeals were made to the instructive facts of the issues of usurpation and oppression, that millions of property had been wantonly destroyed by British hirelings and mercenary troops, that individual rights and possessions had been disregarded, that the records of churches, of institutions of learning, and the libraries of schools and colleges, had been consumed. A further glance at affairs presented the fact, that conflicting and erroneous statements of the war itself, and of the primary motives of action of its American leaders, were also perverted and tauntingly promulgated as true history by foreign writers. The champions of freedom were daily harassed. To be subjected to such a state of things, was no more nor less than to yield to renewed degradation, and to leave the contest an im perfect work. In fine, the tares which had been rooted out were, it was apprehended, again to infest the soil, and liberty itself again to be endangered.

Topics involving matters of this nature were not unfrequently the subjects of warm controversy. The people were cognizant of the ordeal through which they had passed. They knew there were still among us men of the same calibre for the hour of peril, as those who had proved themselves valiant indeed. They also recognized among us men who saw how difficult in the future would be the procurement of authentic documents for that volume, which, in after times, was destined to prove a second Revelation to man, unless a proper and timely spirit was awaked by co-operation with living witnesses, with those who best knew the price of freedom by the cost of purchase, and who were duly apprised of the value of correct knowledge diffused among a new-born nation. The blood that had been spilt, the lives that had been lost, the treasures that had been expended, were familiar truths of impressive force. But the memorials of a tyrannic government were still more palpable, in the destruction which laid waste so many places, and which encompassed the city round about. And what spectator, however indifferent, could fail to learn by such demonstrations, and cherish in his bosom profitable meditations. I am speaking now, more especially, of the scenes presented in this city. But more than this. New York, which throughout her whole progress has been faithful to constitutional law, and may examine with a bold front her conduct both in peace and in war, had furnished noble intellect and strong muscle in the vast work of colonial disfranchizement. She could boast of patriots who now found their homes as citizens among us, in the residence of their choice. The Clintons, the Livingstons, the Morrises, Jays—Hamilton, Fish, Gates, Steuben, M'Dougal, Rufus King, Duer, Ward, Williamson, Clarkson, Varick, Pendleton, and hundreds of others, who had done service in the times that tried men's souls, were now domiciliated here. How often have I cast a lingering look at many of these worthies in their movements through the public ways, during the earlier period of this city, with here and there a Continental tricornered hat over their venerable fronts, a sight no less gratifying to the beholder than the fragrant wild rose scattered through the American forest. I am not now to tell you what species of knowledge these men diffused among the people, and what doctrines on liberty they espoused; versed as they were in the school of experience, they could utter nothing but wisdom. Suffice it to remark, that they led to that accumulation of manuscripts of revolutionary documents, with which your library is especially enriched.

Other circumstances urged the propriety of organizing some institution which might enhance the patriotic object of a broad foundation, available for the promotion of historical knowledge. It has been demonstrated in numerous instances, as I have in part intimated, that the story of our Revolution, if ever honestly related, must be derived from domestic sources, and from the informed mind of the country. The prejudice abroad which had nullified facts, as in the proceedings instituted to suppress the work of Dr. Ramsey, and cut off its circulation in Europe; the war of crimination which originated from General Burgoyne's publications; the difficulties which arose from Sir Henry Clinton's statements; the Gallaway letters and documents, all could be cited in proof of the expediency. And when still further it was ascertained that Gordon's work, on which such strong hopes were fixed, arising not only from the general reputation of the writer, but strengthened by a knowledge of the opportunities he enjoyed for information, and the labor and devotion he had paid to his subject; when, I remark, it was ascertained that that work was subjected to purification by British authority, because it contained aspersions (so called) on the British character, that it recorded too many atrocious truths to assimilate well with the digestive functions of John Bull; further, that audacious threats were held out that, if published as written by the honest author, from its faithful representations of the acts of many of the renowned characters of the British army and navy, it would lead to libel upon libel, damages upon damages, and thus impoverish the writer, as truth ever so well grounded, even if permitted to be adduced, could not, according to statute, plead in mitigation, thus defeating that integrity at which Gordon had arrived; facts of this notorious nature, comprehended even by the masses, could be productive of no other result than strengthen the general opinion that the American mind must be up and doing, if ever the seal of truth was to stamp her imprimatur on the history of the American Revolution.*

Our friend Pintard repeatedly gave wings to these abuses of foreign writers, as preparatory to his movements for an historical society. He was too full of knowledge, both by observation and by reading, not to feel himself doubly armed on the subject, and your intelligent Librarian, Mr. Moore, can point out to you how ample is your collection of volumes on the Indian, the French, and the Revolutionary wars, chiefly brought together by the zeal and research of your enlightened founder.

Will you allow me now to come more closely at home, and offer a few remarks on the occurrences in our midst, which in the end swelled the tide of popu-

* Dr. Waterhouse, in his work on Junius and his Letters, has very explicitly given us a brief statement of these nefarious transactions. I quote from his preliminary view the following extract: "A very valuable and impartial history of the *American Revolution* was written by the *Rev. William Gordon, D. D.*, an Englishman; who resided about twelve years in Massachusetts, and had access to the best authorities, including that of Washington, Greene, Knox, and Gates, and the journals of Congress and of the Legislatures of the several States. He injudiciously returned to England, there to print his interesting history. He deemed it prudent to submit his manuscript to a gentleman learned in the law, to mark such chapters and passages as might endanger prosecution, when the lawyer returned it with such a large portion expurgated as to reduce about four volumes to three. The author being too aged and too infirm to venture upon a voyage back to America, and too poor withal, he submitted to its publication in a mutilated state; and thus the most just and impartial history of the American war, and of the steps that led to it, on both sides of the Atlantic, was sadly marred, and shamefully mutilated. My authority is from my late venerable friend *John Adams*, the President of these United States, who perused Gordon's manuscript when he was our Minister at the Court of London, and from my own knowledge, having been shown a considerable portion of the History before the author left this country to die in his own, and having corresponded with him till near the close of his long life."

lar feeling in behalf of your institution. "No people in the world," says a late lamented citizen, Herman E. Ludwig, can have so great an interest in the history of their country, as those of the United States of North America; "for there are none," adds this learned German, "who enjoy an equally great share in their country's historical acts." Glorious New York has, from the beginning of her career down to the present hour, ever been the theatre of thought, of action, and of results, and so I presume she is to continue. Her adventurous character has rendered her the acknowledged pioneer of the Republic, and her thousand examples of improved policy in municipal affairs, in building, in domestic economy, in the several departments of arts and of commerce, have yielded by their adoption blessings untold to other cities of the Union. From the time of that great improvement, as it was called, the construction of side walks for foot passengers in the streets, only one hundred and thirty-four years after the streets themselves were first paved, (a long Rip Van Winkle torpor,) at which service we find Pintard struggled with the corporate authorities in 1791–2, down to that mighty achievement, the introduction of the Croton water, by the genius of Douglass, she has been the exemplar for other cities of the Republic, and approved by the enlightened foreigner who has visited our shores, from every nation.

Common observation has repeatedly confirmed the fact, that the greatest and the smallest events are often synchronous. With the birth of the Revolution of France in 1789, I made my first appearance on this planet, and the arrival of the Ambuscade four years after, from the notoriety of the event and its consequences, enables me to bring to feeble recollection many of the scenes which transpired in this city at that time: the popular excitement and bustle, the liberty cap, the entrée of citizen Genet, the Red Cockade, the song of the carmagnole, in which with childish ambition I united, the rencontre with the Boston frigate, and the commotion arising from Jay's treaty. Though I cannot speak earnestly from actual knowledge, we must all concede that these were the times when political strife assumed a formidable aspect, when the press most flagrantly outraged individual rights and domestic peace—that the impugners of the Washington administration received new weapons with which to inflict their assaults upon tried patriotism, by every arrival from abroad, announcing France in her progress. The federalists and the anti-federalists now became the federal and the republican party: the carmagnole sung every hour of every day in the streets, and on stated days at the Belvidere Club House, fanned the embers and enkindled that zeal which caused the overthrow of many of the soundest principles of American freedom. Even the yellow fever, which from its novelty and its malignancy struck terror in every bosom, and was rendered more lurid by the absurd preventive means of burning tar and tar barrels in almost every street, afforded no mitigation of party animosity, and Greenleaf with his Argus, Freneau with his Time Piece, and Cobbett with his Porcupine Gazette, increased the consternation which only added to the inquietude of the peaceable citizen who had often reasoned within himself, that a seven years' carnage, through which he had passed, had been enough for one life. The arrogance of party-leaders was alike acrimonious toward their opponents, and reasoning on every side seemed equally nugatory. Nor could Tammany, ostensibly the patron saint of aboriginal antiquities, calm the multitudinous waves of faction, though her public processions were decorated with the insignia of the calumet, and the song of peace was chanted in untold strains accompanied by the Goddess of Liberty, with discolored countenance and Indian trappings, and patriotic citizens, such as Josiah Ogden Hoffman, Cadwallader D. Colden and William Mooney, as sachems, with many others, followed in her train.

I have not the rashness to invade the chair on which is seated with so much national benefit and renown the historian Bancroft, nor approach the sphere of the historical orator of the nation, Edward Everett; still, as your association is historical in all its aims, I shall present a few additional circumstances which signalized the spirit of those memorable times in New York. Much I saw—much has been told me by the old inhabitants, now departed. When the entire American nation, nay, when the civilized world at large seemed electrified by the outbreak of the revolution of France, it necessarily followed, as the shadow does the substance, that the American soul, never derelict, could not but enkindle with patriotic warmth at the cause of that people whose loftiest desire was freedom; of that people who themselves had, with profuse appropriation, enabled that very bosom, in the moment of hardest trial, to inhale the air of liberty. Successive events had now dethroned the monarchy of France, and the democratic spirit was now evolved in its fullest element. It was not surprising that the experienced and the sober champions who had effected the great revolution of the Colonies should now make the cause of struggling France their own; and as victors already in one desperate crisis, they seemed ready to enter into a new contest for the rights of man. The masses coalesced and co-operated. Cheering prospects of sympathy and of support were held out in the prospective to their former friends and benefactors abroad. Jealousy of Britain, affection for France, was now the prevailing impulse, and the business of the day was often interrupted by tumultuous noises in the streets. Groups of sailors might be collected on the docks and at the shipping ready to embark on a voyage of plunder; merchants and traders in detached bodies might be seen discussing the hazards of commerce; the schools liberated from their prescribed hours of study, because of some fresh report of the Ambuscade or of Genet, the schoolmaster uttering in his dismissal a new reason for the study of the classics, by expounding with oracular dignity to his scholars, *Vivat Respublica*, now broadly printed as the caption of the play-bill or the pamphlet just issued. The crew of the French frigate moored off Peck Slip, were now disgorged on shore, and organizing to march in file, increased by many natives, bearing the liberty cap with reverence to the residence of the French Consul, in Water street, and thence proceeding to the Bowling Green, patriotically to root out, by paving stones thrown in showers, the debris of the old statue of George III. The tri-color was in every hand or affixed to every watch-chain, while from every lip was vociferated the carmagnole. Meanwhile the two old notorious arch-tories, who had fattened on lies and libels, and before whose doors the procession passed, were snugly ensconced behind their shop counter;

Rivington in rich purple velvet coat, full wig and cane, and ample frills, dealing out good stationery to his customers; and Gaine, in less ostentatious costume, ready with religious zeal to dispose of his recent edition of the Book of Common Prayer to all true worshippers.

Political clubs abounded everywhere. The fraternity of the two nations was the great theme. They deliberated on the doctrine of Lafayette in the National Assembly—"When oppression renders a revolution necessary, insurrection is the most sacred of duties." The democratic principle assumed a more vigorous form, and the Democratic Society, the first in this city, and perhaps the first in the Union, was organized, with Henry Rutgers, an affluent and distinguished citizen, as its president.

But the time was near at hand when this flood in revolutionary affairs was about to find its ebb, so far as concerned the universal sympathy which America had cherished for struggling France. She had contemplated the overthrow of the monarchy, the destruction of the privileged orders, the execution of the king, with more or less approval; and, from the freedom of the press, and the diffusion of knowledge, our citizens were perhaps as copiously enlightened in the transactions of Paris as most of the inhabitants of that capital in the midst of all its doings. But fresher and still more portentous intelligence now poured in among us. All knew that the tree of liberty had been planted in human blood; yet the delights at its growth were sometimes checked by the means of its nutrition. Nor was this virtiginous state of public opinion long to last. Some of the hitherto most factious and sturdy jacobinical advocates took alarm at the rapid march of foreign events. In the public assemblies graver deliberations filled the speaker's mind, and the fulminations of anarchy gave way to the persuasive logic of rule and right. History was now, indeed, teaching philosophy. So far as concerned the war itself, nothing abroad so effectively chilled the ardor of the American people as the sanguinary measures of Robespierre, while at home the extraordinary career of Genet increased the dissatisfaction to the cause of Republican France, and added to the anxiety which the predominance of jacobinical principles might occasion.

Amidst these momentous events, others scarcely less alarming were seen approaching, aggravated by the rebellious tendencies of foreign interference and the malign career of Genet,* the lawless spirit of the times, and the increase of popular disaffection towards Eng-

* I have spoken of Genet with severity: he labors under reproach by every historian who has recorded his deeds, and by none is he more chastised than by Judge Marshall; yet withal, Genet possessed a kindly nature, was exuberant in speech, of lively parts, and surcharged with anecdotes. His intellectual culture was considerable; he was master of several living languages, a proficient in music as well as a skilful performer. To a remark I made to him touching his execution on the piano, he subjoined: "I have given many hours daily for twelve years to this instrument, and now reach some effective sounds." He had a genius for mechanics, and after he had become an agriculturalist in this country, wrote on machinery and on husbandry. He assured me (in 1812) the time would arrive when his official conduct as minister would be cleared of its dark shades. To other shoulders, said he, will be transferred the odium I now bear. In a conversation with him on the vicissitudes and events of the French Revolution, he said, "Their leaders were novices: had they been versed in Albany politics but for three months, we would have escaped many trials, and our patriotism been crowned with better results." It is to be regretted that the papers of Genet have not yet seen the light: they embrace letters from Voltaire and Rousseau, and years' correspondence of eminent American statesmen down to the close of his eventful life. He died at Jamaica, Long Island, in 1834, aged 71 years.

land. The appointment of Jay as minister extraordinary to Great Britain, the debates in Congress on the Treaty which he had negotiated, and the local turmoil which found encouragement elsewhere as well as in this city, are facts strongly within the memory of the venerable men still alive among us. As might be inferred, the provisions of the treaty were assaulted with the greatest vehemence by jacobinical or democratic clubs, and the disciples of the most spotless of patriots decried in language which can scarcely find a parallel in the vocabulary of abuse. The disorganizing multitude, segregated in divers parts of the town, soon found a rallying point at the Bowling Green, opposite to the Government House, and signalized themselves by burning a copy of the Treaty amidst the wildest shrieks of demoniac fury,—while some of the Livingstons, (among whom the most grateful associations clustered for revolutionary services in behalf of dear America,) with more than thoughtless effrontery fanned the embers of discontent, and William S. Smith (a son-in-law of old President Adams) presided with magisterial importance at a formidable meeting of the malcontents, who passed resolutions deprecatory of the stipulations of the negotiation and of the principles and acts espoused by the advocates of the great measure. To give a still more alarming aspect to affairs, Hamilton and Rufus King, occupying the balcony of the City Hall, in Wall street, and addressing the people in accents of friendship and peace and reconciliation, were treated in return by showers of stones levelled at their persons by the exasperated mob gathered in front of that building. These are hard arguments to encounter, exclaimed the noble-hearted Hamilton. Edward Livingston, (afterwards so celebrated for his Louisianian Code,) was, I am informed, one of this violent number. What Washington called a counter-current, however, actually took place at a meeting of the old Chamber of Commerce, at the head of which was Comfort Sands, an experienced man who had been long before a member of the Committee of Safety in the days of the Liberty Boys. This important body on trade and commerce voted resolutions declaring their approbation of the treaty. But let me refer you to the history of that time-honored association written by Charles King, LL. D., for further particulars.

I believe old Tammany was then too intent in effecting their original design, with their charter before them, of gathering together the relics of nature, art, beads, wampum, tomahawks, belts, earthen jugs and pots, and other Indian antiquities, with all that could be found of Indian literature in war songs, and in hieroglyphical barks, to take any special movement in this crisis of public solicitude for the safety of the Union. Tammany, to her honor, adhered together by a strong conservative Americanism, and stood aloof from the influence of foreign contamination. That these assertions are founded on more than conjecture, is deducible from contemporaneous events. One of the beloved idols among their members, was the erudite Dr. Samuel Latham Mitchill. Early after the organization of the society, he discoursed before the Society of Black Friars, on the character of St. Tammany, the Incas of Peru, and the benignant aspect of our Republic. Nothing had reference to our domestic trials. Still later, at a season of much agitation among us, as Sachem, in another address on the Red Man of the New World, he congratulated the members on their patron saint, with the hope that their squaws and papooses were all well.

Public opinion, as I have already intimated, had become somewhat doubtful as to the wisdom which marked the French revolution. Many, once seemingly secure in the light of nature alone, now felt themselves led into a delusion, the results of which threatened more than temporal inconvenience. The middle and the best classes of society, the responsible citizen, who had at one time fraternized with these apostles of liberty, now foresaw that certain doctrines engrafted on and interwoven with the political dogmas of the day, were more serious in their intent than avowed, and penetrated deeper into the inward parts than the stripes of partisan leaders and the acts of military chieftains. Equivocation only rendered more noxious the skepticism which was too prominently rearing its head. Few were so blind as not to see that infidelity, wrapt in the mantle of the sovereign rights of the people, indulged the hope of her triumphant establishment, and the downfall of the strongest pillars of the Christian faith.

As the darkness which had shrouded the actual state of things broke away, new light shone upon the conduct of the revolutionists. A devouter feeling was in progress, and circumstances were better comprehended. The Gospel of charity, of peace, and of good will to all men, it was safely inferred, was not to be advanced by existing transactions, nor its dignity elucidated with advantage by the foulest blasphemies. It was further seen that the pestilential exhalations of Paris had not merely polluted all France, but that they had widely diffused themselves throughout the Continent; that Germany had her Illuminati; that England breathed the noxious vapor with spasmodic vehemence; that Scotland was tainted; that Ireland was ready for a change of elemental life.

Enough had now transpired abroad to awaken alarm at home. New York, which, to her everlasting honor be it said, had been founded and reared under her original settlers, the Dutch, and with the exception of some slight misrule on the part of her English masters (see our faithful and distinguished historian Brodhead *), had uniformly sustained religious toleration down to the present moment; New York, which had with the nobleness of freemen looked with sympathizing eyes on revolutionary France in her incipient warfare on behalf of a persecuted and trodden-down nation, could no longer continue incredulous as to the mischief and abuse which afflicted others, nor skeptical as to the disorder and moral degradation which threatened even her own domestic fireside.

"A change came o'er the spirit of her dream."

I have said already that her revolutionary heroes wavered in their hopes that our people were swayed by anticipated benefits; that the political clubs took alarm; that, in short, among men of all orders and professions, Doubting Castle stood before them. Liberty, the attractive goddess, once decorated in her robes of resplendent purity, was now transformed into an hideous monstrosity. The professing Christians

* History of the State of New York: by John Romeyn Brodhead. First period 1609–1664. New York: Harper & Brothers, 8vo., 1853.

stood aghast when they learned that abroad every tenth day was appointed for the Sabbath; that death was pronounced an eternal sleep: that it was resolved by the Corresponding Society of Paris that the belief of a God was so pernicious an opinion, as to be an exception to the general principle of toleration. The clergy, with us, could no longer withstand these atrocious sentiments. "Better," said they, "abandon the cause of liberty, once so dear to our humanity, than adhere to it at such a sacrilegious cost. Better abandon France than abandon our God." The balance was struck, and many of that exalted order of men who had been the advocates of the revolution, were now turned and became its most implacable enemies. William Linn, of the Collegiate Dutch Church, an eminent divine and accomplished preacher, was of the number of the converts. He had published the Signs of the Times in behalf of Liberty and France; his troubled bosom now gave relief to itself by his Discourse on National Sins. The Voice of Warning, a powerful Discourse by a popular man, John M Mason, was also widely circulated. The party feuds which had annoyed real believers of different denominations on such points as adult and pædo-baptism, on certain rituals, on ordination and the like, and which had hitherto been the only obstacle to the more earnest and greater extension of religious conformity by the clergy of different sects, were apprehended now as merely nothing, in comparison to the evils which seemed impending. The tranquillity of the whole clerical body stood on the borders of destruction. The prelacy was alarmed, and the so-called dissenters of every faith were ill at ease. They had felt the whirlwind, they now dreaded the storm. The wolf threatened to destroy both the shepherd and his flock. The pulpit, so often and so effectively the means of relief of private sorrow, now waged uncompromising war with her thunderbolts from heaven, to rescue that only precious book, as Mason called the Bible, from the consuming influence of atheism.

I am not to measure the extent of the benefits conferred by the ministry at that dark time when ominous formalities in the streets awakened the public gaze, when the ears were distracted by terrible blasphemy, and folly and infidelity had reached their climax; but when I know that that majestic father of theology, Dr. Livingston, of the Dutch Reformed Church, Dr. Rodgers and Dr. John M. Mason, of the Presbyterian community, that learned dignitary of the Episcopate, Bishop Provoost; John Foster, of the Baptists; Francis Asbury, of the Methodists, and Kunze of the German Lutheran Church, were of the number, and were enumerated among the best of men who encountered the times and openly declared their faith, in order to rescue the people from themselves; I feel bound to infer that some of the lepers must have been cleansed. That eyesight was not received by all, and the scoffers not altogether silenced, the history of that period gives us painful proofs. That you may understand me the better, I will weary your patience a moment longer with a few circumstances which fell under the observation of every attentive person at that period. Nor will you accuse me of invective while I recite the story.

I believe it is set down as a political axiom that war is not conducive to the progress of religious belief.

Be this as it may, our revolutionary contest in its wide-spread desolation had left the institutions of learning and of theology encompassed with perils and in the lowest temporal condition. Time was requisite to restore their ability and their influence; and ecclesiastical affairs necessarily halted in their march, from the penury which pervaded the country and the overburdened cares of a people, full of gratitude at their liberation from the yoke of tyranny, yet hardly ready to summon the requisite means for such important and grave ends. In the meanwhile, the conclusion must be made that a sprinkling of philosophical belief, in contradistinction to that of religious, had here and there penetrated the public mind and entered the soil of liberty, derived from the already scattered circulation of the writings of Voltaire, Helvetius, Rousseau, and the Encyclopædists. But the land was doomed to be still deeper impregnated and the dwellers thereon to partake in larger bounty of the products of a new husbandry, the fruits of a new revelation, in the enjoyment of which nature, rejecting absurdities and rejoicing in a higher knowledge, would understand her own powers and assert her inherent dignity. The work was therefore not entirely abortive, when, upon the arrival of the Ambuscade within our waters, was also brought that material which constructed the Temple of Reason and led numerous worshippers to her shrine. The Theophilanthropists reared their heads, and Deistical Clubs were in formative operation. However repellent to the doctrines of a religion which, with uprightness of intention and the deepest conviction, the people at large maintained in conscious purity; however antagonistic to that faith which they had in infancy been taught and in riper years cherished as their greatest blessing, their allegiance to the God of their fathers was nevertheless in many instances neutralized by the poison they imbibed, and in many cases broken asunder by pretexts of superior enlightenment—a more tenable rationality, the pride of intellect. That these philosophical teachers well comprehended the avenues of triumph over the human heart, is now understood better than in the days of their active labors. At that period of our city's growth, scholastic knowledge was but sparingly diffused among us, and the manageable multitude were easily led captive by the dexterity of Jacobinical instructors, who knew how to accommodate their lessons to the affections of the unenlightened and untaught. Besides which, liberty and the rights of man were so insidiously interwoven with the fallacies of skepticism, that while the former vouchsafed the dearest privileges, the latter was so masked that numbers unawares were indoctrinated and became the disciples of the theistical school. These clandestine movements were not without their consequences in other sections of the State, more especially at and about Newburgh, in the county of Orange. That county had been known as the residence of a fierce democracy for some time. It was patriotic in revolutionary times, and its political sentiments generally ran high. It was destined afterwards to become the scene of the Druidical Society, for so the free-thinkers nominated their fraternity. They feigned the principles of the Illuminati and of the Jacobin Clubs. They alternately conducted their public worship in New York and at Newburgh; and at this latter place I have assurances that the typical symbols of Christianity were sometimes outrageously profaned.

I might mention the names of several of the leading officials of this confederacy, were this the occasion, —with a number of them I afterwards became well acquainted in my professional life. There were talents and knowledge among them, and an ardent thirst for liberty: they had warm hearts, strong affections, but lacked the conservative and wholesome principles on which a republic must depend for its prosperity and duration. I would draw a veil over the closing scenes of some of their lives. How often we behold a mystery! The county which had given to Noah Webster the school-house in which he first imparted juvenile knowledge, and where he first concocted the famous Spelling-book which has since given instruction and morality to millions of the youth of both sexes of this nation, became in the progress of events the patron of a society whose every act seemed destined to demolish those very principles on which both liberty and life depend.

In the midst of these commotions, certain presses were not tardy in the diffusion of works favoring the great designs of infidelity: Condorcet and Volney, Tindall and Boulanger, became accessible in libraries and circulated widely by purchase. But no work had a demand for readers at all comparable to that of Paine, and it is a fact almost incredible that the Age of Reason, on its first appearance in this city, was printed as an orthodox book, by orthodox publishers, of a house of orthodox faith, doubtless deceived by the vast renown which the author of Common Sense had obtained, and the prospects of sale; acting on the principle given in the Cyclopœdia, in its definition of a good book, in booksellers' language, "one that sells well." The same publishers, however, made early atonement for their bibliographical error, in their immense circulation of Watson's Apology.

We had in those days other commotions touching articles of belief of another order of delusion. I mean the promulgation of the rhapsodies of Richard Brothers, who affirmed he had received a special gift, and who in England had aroused attention by his revelations and prophetic visions not altogether unlike those of the Millerites of the other day in this metropolis. David Austin, of New Jersey, came hither to our relief, and occupying a prominent pulpit denounced Brothers as a deceiver, imparting his own learned disquisitions on the millennium; while Townley, a worthy man and laborious expositor, the last in the city of that denomination of preachers of the old Oliver Cromwell belief, in a neighboring edifice was expounding the "unsearchable riches," and demonstrating the decrees of infinite wisdom by enlightening his audience with a burning candle on his desk, in which I observed he protruded his medial finger in order to elucidate that passage of holy writ, "when thou walkest in the fire, thou shalt not be consumed, and the flame shall not burn thee."

The great instrument in the promotion of deistical doctrines during that singular period in New York, was Elihu Palmer, a speaker of much earnestness, whose pulmonary apparatus gave force to a deep, sonorous and emphatic utterance. He was a native of Connecticut, born in 1763, was graduated at Dartmouth College, brought up a Congregationalist—assumed the ministry, but after a short period was suddenly transformed into a Deist. In his study he was reading the psalm, translated by Watts, "Lord, I am vile, conceived in sin." He doubted, he denied the declaration; he abandoned preaching. Riker, in his valuable Annals of Newtown, gives an interesting detail of the circumstances. Palmer proceeded to Philadelphia for the purpose of the study and practice of the law, took the yellow fever of 1793, became totally blind, and gave up his law pursuits. He now in right earnestness assumed the function of a deistical preacher in this city, in 1796. He died in Philadelphia of pleurisy, in the winter of 1805 or 1806. In what manner he added to the stores of his wisdom after his loss of sight, I know not; but must infer that his associate followers became in turns readers to him. His information, from early inquiry and a strong love of knowledge, with the means referred to, secured to him the title of a man of parts; such was the general reputation he bore. I have more than once listened to Palmer; none could be weary within the sound of his voice; his diction was classical, and much of his natural theology attractive by variety of illustration. But admiration often sunk into despondency at his assumption, and his sarcastic assaults on things most holy. His boldest philippic was his discourse on the title page of the Bible, in which, with the double shield of jacobinism and infidelity, he warned rising America against confidence in a book authorized by the monarchy of England, and inveighed against royalty and the treacherous James, with at least equal zeal as did that sensualist issue his Counterblast against the most innocent recreation that falls within the scope of weary mortals. Palmer delivered his sermons in the Union Hotel, in William street.

His audience was composed of a large body of the free-thinkers of that day His Principles of Nature, a 12mo, was reprinted in London about the time of the Thistlewood riots. Palmer's strongest personal friends were John Fellowes, an author of some volumes; Rose, an unfortunate lawyer; Taylor, a philanthropist, and Charles Christian.

During the later years of his pastoral functions, as he called them, he was aided by a co-laborer in another part of the city, of physical proportions even more stately, of still more daring speech, whose voice was as the surge of mighty billows, whose jacobinism was, if possible, still fiercer; I allude to John Foster: I have heard many speakers, but none whose voice ever equalled the volume of Foster's. It flowed with delicious ease, and yet penetrated every where. He besides was favored with a noble presence. Points of difference existed in their theological dogmas, yet they had the same ends in view; radicalism and the spread of the jacobinical element. Foster's exordium consisted generally in an invocation to the goddess of liberty, now unshackled, who inhaled nutrition from heaven, seated on her throne of more than Alpine heights. Palmer and Foster called each other brother, and the fraternity was most cordial. I have sometimes thought, could we find more frequently the same strenuous efforts as these men employed, called into action by that exalted order of persons whose aim is the diffusion of evangelical truth, we should also find a wider extension of the gospel dispensation. Methinks there is a deficiency somewhere:

> " 'Tis of ourselves that we are thus or thus:
> Our bodies are our gardens, to the which
> Our minds are gardeners."

But the programme of our theological warfare in those remarkable times is not yet complete. While these scenes were enacting, there were other establishments not idle. The society of friends, peaceable as from the beginning, held their service in the Pearl street and Liberty street meeting-houses; not as yet disturbed by the innovations on primitive Barclay, introduced by Elias Hicks, an able preacher of strong reasoning powers, and which subsequently agitated that religious community from the city of their American origin through various states of the Union; yet, in the end, unavailable to suppress that inward comfort (as Penn calls it) "which leads the soul to silent converse with heaven, and prompts to acts of beneficence for suffering mortals."

The Universalists, with Edward Mitchell and William Palmer, though circumscribed in fiscal means, nevertheless drew together a most respectable body of believers to their house of worship in Magazine street. They were both men of eloquence and good pleaders in behalf of their tenets, and had large auditories. Occasionally they were sustained in the work of their conviction by the preaching of John Murray, an Englishman by birth, whose casual absence from his people in Massachusetts enabled him to gratify the disciples of their creed in New York. Murray had a rival of a like name to his own, of the Calvinistic faith, a man of sound erudition and rhetorical powers, and in contradistinction they were designated by the sobriquet Salvation and Damnation Murray. These men moved together so harmoniously, that they often alternately occupied the same pulpit, on the same day, in New England. The Universalist, little John Murray, had much of the primitive about him; his rich humility, his grave accent, and his commentaries on the divine love, won him distinction from every discourse. None could withhold a kindly approbation. He seemed to me always to be charged with tracts on benevolence, and distributing a periodical called the Berean, or Scripture Searcher. He called himself a Berean.

The doctrines of the Universalists had been entertained and promulgated in New York and elsewhere among Americans, long prior to the time of the public discourses of Mitchell and Palmer. Chauncey's book had been read by thousands; William Pitt Smith, a doctor of physic, and a professor of materia medica in Columbia College, in this city, had published his Letters of Amyntor; Winchester's Lectures on Universal Restoration and on the Prophecies, had been circulated with a strong recommendatory letter in their belief from the pen of Dr. Rush; and Huntington's Calvinism Improved, or the Gospel Illustrated as a System of Real Grace issuing in the Salvation of all Men, had gained much notoriety from the peculiar circumstances which accompanied its publication as a posthumous work, and the able reply to it by the celebrated Dr. Strong, of Hartford. We moreover had a slender volume on the same topic from a medical prescriber in this city, by the name of Young. Seed therefore had been sown broadcast, ere Mitchell had mounted the pulpit. Nevertheless, the Universalists may look back with equal emotions of gratitude at the labors of Mitchell and Palmer for a series of years in their service, begun some fifty years ago, while their society was in its infancy, as at the present day they hail their accomplished orator, Dr. Chapin, as their ecclesiastical leader.

What a beautiful and instructive example of toleration is set forth in this brief history of forms of belief!

I had the opportunity, in the Magazine street church, of listening to a discourse full of personal observation and reminiscences, from the lips of Stewart, the Walking Philosopher, as the books call him; a man of altitude, whose inferior limbs provided him with peculiar facilities to visit almost every part of the earth as a pedestrian, before we had railways, and who enlightened his audience with descriptive touches of Egypt and her pyramids, of Nova Zembla, "and the Lord knows where." I shall never forget his unostentatious, though impressive appearance; his lank figure, his long neck, his long nose, his wide mouth, and his broad white hat.

There is one other subject I must place within the background of this picture of past times, and that is street preaching. The older inhabitants tell us we had much of it in the earlier condition of this city, shortly after the inauguration of the first President of the United States. I remember well repeated examples of this sort of edification in the public ways. I shall specify but one, and that was to be found in the person of Lorenzo Dow. Dow was a Wesleyan, of rare courage and determined zeal. He scarcely ever presented himself without drawing together large multitudes of hearers, in part owing to his grotesque appearance, but not a little arising from his dexterous elocution and his prompt vocabulary. He was faithful to his mission, and a benefactor to Methodism in that day. His weapons against Beelzebub were providential interpositions, wondrous disasters, touching sentiments, miraculous escapes, something after the method of John Bunyan. His religious zeal armed him with Christian forbearance, while his convictions allowed him a justifiable use of the strongest flagellations for besetting sins. Sometimes you were angered by his colloquial vulgarity; but he never descended so low as Huntington, the sinner saved, the blasphemous coal-heaver of England. He was rather a coarse edition on brown paper, with battered type, of Rowland Hill. Like the disciplined histrionic performer, he often adjusted himself to adventitious circumstances; in his field exercises, at camp meetings, and the like, a raging storm might be the forerunner of God's immediate wrath; a change of element might betoken Paradise restored, or a new Jerusalem. He had genius at all times to construct a catastrophe. His apparent sincerity and his indubitable earnestness sustained and carried him onward, while many ran to and fro. Repartee, humor, wit, irony, were a portion of his stock in trade, the materials he adroitly managed. Sometimes he was redundant in love and the affections, at other times acrimonious and condemnatory. Altogether Lorenzo was an original, and a self-sustained man, and would handle more than the rhetorician's tools. His appearance must have occasionally proved a drawback to his argument, but he was resolute and heroic. His garments, like his person, seemed to have little to do with the detersive influence of cleanliness. With dishevelled locks of black flowing hair over his shoulders, like Edward Irving of many tongues, and a face which, like the fashion of our own day, rarely ever knew a razor, his piercing gray eyes of rapid mobility, infiltrated with a glabrous moisture, rolled with a keen perception, and was the frequent index of his mental armory. I have implied that he was always ready at a rejoinder; an instance or two may be given: A dissenter from Dow's Arminian doctrines, after listening to his harangue, asked him if he knew what Calvinism was? "Yes," he promptly replied:—

'You can and you can't,
You will and you won't;
You'll be damned if you do,
And you'll be damned if you don't.'

That, sir, is Calvinism, something more than rhyme." I, who have rarely left New York for a day during the past fifty years, was in the summer of 1824 at Utica with an invalid patient. It so happened that Dow, at that very time, held forth in an adjacent wood, having for his audience some of the Oneida and Reservation Indians, together with a vast assemblage of the people of Utica and the neighboring villages. Mounted on an advantageous scaffolding, he discoursed on the rewards of a good life and pictured the blessings of heaven. Upon his return to the hotel there was found among the occupants a Mr. Branch and old General Root, so familiarly known for the opprobrious name of "the Big Ditch," which he gave to Clinton's Canal. These two gentlemen addressed Dow, told him they had heard him say much of heaven, and now begged to ask him if he would describe the place. "Yes," says Dow, with entire ease. "Heaven is a wide and expansive region, a beautiful plain, something like our prairie country—without any thing to obstruct the vision—there is neither Root nor Branch there." Dow had one great requisite for a preacher; he feared no man. There were but two houses of public worship of the Methodist Society when I first heard him, the first erected in John Street, with old Peter Williams, the tobacconist, as sexton. The old negro was then striving to sustain a rival opposition in the tobacco line, with the famous house of the Lorillards. The other meeting-house was in Second, now Forsyth street. In this latter I have listened to Dow from the pulpit, with his wife Peggy near him, a functionary of equally attractive personal charms. A reciprocal union of heads and hearts seemed to bind them together. We are not to forget that Moorsfield was mad when Lorenzo Dow was an itinerant spiritual instructor with us; and who shall now estimate the advance of that vast denomination of Christians from that period, with the solitary and starveling magazine of William Phœbus as the exponent of its doctrines, up to its present commanding condition, with the venerable names of Hedding, Fisk, Durbin, Olin, Simpson and Stevens, among its recorded apostles, with its rich and affluent periodical literature, its well-endowed schools and colleges, its myriad of churches, its soul-sustaining melodious hymns, its astounding Book Concern, with its historian Bangs, and its erudite M'Clintock among its great theological professors and authors.

If my memory fails me not, in the month of May, 1819, arrived in this city William Ellery Channing, with a coadjutor, both distinguished preachers of the Unitarian persuasion, of Boston. They were solicitous to procure a suitable place of worship. They made application at churches of different denominations of religious belief, to be accommodated at the intermediate hours between the morning and afternoon service, but in vain. They next urged their request at several of the public charities where convenient apartments might be found, but with the same result. Like the two saints in Baucis and Philemon—

> "Tried every tone might pity win,
> But not a soul would let them in."

Still not wholly disheartened, a communication was received from them, through a committee, addressed to the trustees of the College of Physicians and Surgeons, then in Barclay street. The Board was forthwith summoned, and the special business of the meeting fully discussed, but with some warmth of feeling. This communication read as follows:—

"*May* 11, 1819.

"To David Hosack, M. D.

"Sir:—It may be known to you that there are individuals in this city who have been accustomed to receive religious instruction from pastors who are not associated with the regular clergy of this place. Some of those gentlemen would be gratified to have it in their power to improve the opportunities for a continuance of this instruction, which are occasionally afforded by the temporary visits of the clergy of their acquaintance to this city.

"The subscribers would, on this occasion, particularly mention that the Rev. Wm. E. Channing, of Boston, is expected to pass the next Sunday with his friends in New York.

"Emboldened by a consciousness of the liberality which distinguishes your enlightened profession, they take the liberty to desire you to lay before the Board of the Medical College their request, that the lecture-room of that institution may be used for the purposes above alluded to. They would confine their request for the present, to the use of the room on the next Sunday, but would venture to suggest that there may probably be future occasions when a repetition of the favor now asked, would be gratefully received, and in such case they would be happy to comply with any terms as to compensation which the College may deem proper.

We are, Sir, with great respect,
Your obedient servants,
I. G. Pearson.
H. D. Sedgwick.
H. D. Sewall.

New York, May 10, 1819."

"Proceedings of the College.

"Letter from I. G. Pearson, H. D. Sedgwick, and Henry D. Sewall, was read:

"Resolved, That this College grant permission to the Rev. W. E. Channing, of Boston, to perform divine service in the Hall of this University on the ensuing Sunday, as requested in the above communication.

"The Registrar of the college, John W. Francis, was authorized to furnish a copy of said resolution to said committee, duly signed by the President of the Board and the Registrar."

On the following Sabbath, Dr. Channing entered the professorial desk of the larger lecture-room, and delivered, in his mellowed accents, a discourse to a crowded audience, among whom were his associate brother preacher, and several professors of the college. But two or three days had transpired, from the occurrence of this first preaching of Unitarianism, before it was loudly spoken of, and in terms of disapprobation not the mildest. The censure on such a pernicious toleration came strongest from the Presbyterian order of clergy. I heard but one prominent Episcopalian condemn the whole affair, but that condemnation was in emphatic phraseology. There doubtless were others. Inquiries were made what individuals had constituted the meeting; and as a majority happened to be the professors of the college, they were particularly destined to receive the hardest blows. Some three days after that memorable Sunday, I accidentally met the great theological thunderbolt of the times, Dr. John M. Mason, in the bookstore of that intelligent publisher and learned bibliopole, James Eastburn. Mason soon approached me, and in earnestness exclaimed, "You doctors have been engaged in a wrongful work; you have permitted heresy to come in among us, and have countenanced its approach. You have furnished accommodations for the devil's disciples." Not wholly unhinged, I replied, "We saw no such great evil in an act of religious toleration; nor do I think," I added, "that one individual member is responsible for the acts of an entire corporation." "You are all equally guilty," cried the doctor, with enkindled warmth. "Do you know what you have done? You have advanced infidelity by complying with the request of these skeptics." "Sir," said I, "we hardly felt disposed to sift their articles of belief as a religious society." "There, sir, there is the difficulty," exclaimed the doctor. "Belief: they have no belief—they believe in nothing, having nothing to believe. They are a paradox; you cannot fathom them: how can you fathom a thing that has no bottom?" I left the doctor dreadfully indignant, uttering something of the old slur on the skeptical tendencies of the faculty of physic. Such was the beginning of Unitarian public worship in this city.

If there be present any of that religious association within the sound of my voice, I throw myself upon their clemency, that they be not offended by my ecclesiastical facts. I aim at a veracious historical narrative of times long elapsed, and I feel that my personal knowledge of many members of that religious persuasion will secure me from inimical animadversion by so enlightened and charitable a denomination. Unitarianism had indeed its advocates among us long before the pilgrimage of Channing in 1819. Every body at all versed in the progress of religious creeds in this country, will, I believe, assign to Dr. James Freeman the distinction of having been the first Unitarian minister of the first Unitarian church in New England. He promulgated his faith from the pulpit of King's Chapel in Boston, which church, however, had been vacant for some time, owing to political circumstances growing out of the American revolution. He thus became the means of converting the first Episcopal church of the New England States into the first Unitarian church. Having been refused ordination by Bishop Provoost of New York, Freeman received a lay ordination by his society alone, as their rector and minister, in 1787. I know nothing of him personally; but the old and the young tell us he was of spotless integrity, of a sweet demeanor, and heavenly minded. He was an active promoter of the Massachusetts Historical Society; he was a correspondent of Lindley and of Belsham. The distinguished Channing, who had been a rigid Calvinist, was converted by Freeman into a Unitarian. John Kirkland, so long the admired President of Harvard University, impressed with like theological doctrines, was sedulous in his calling, and earnest in making known the "Light of Nature," a work of curious metaphysical research from the acute mind of Abraham Tucker, published under the assumed name of Edward Search.

That our Boston friends had favored us with disciples of that faith in this city before that time is most certain, else a society of that order of believers could not have been so rapidly formed as appears by their organization in Chambers street in 1821, when the Rev. Edward Everett delivered the dedication sermon, with suitable exercises by the Rev. Henry Ware, jun.; again, at the installation of their new building, corner of Prince and Mercer streets, in 1826, when Dr. Channing preached the dedication sermon, and the Rev. Dr. Walker offered the final prayer. Still further, we find the Church of the Messiah, in Broadway, consecrated and the installation sermon delivered by Dr. Walker, and the pastoral duties assigned to Dr. Dewey; but, for some years past, these have been discharged by Dr. Osgood. And again, we find the organization of the Church of the Divine Unity completed in 1845, the pastoral duties devolving on Dr. Bellows; and again, the last-named church being disposed of to the Universalist Society, we witness the magnificent edifice for Unitarian worship, called All Souls' Church, situated on the Fourth Avenue, consecrated December 25, 1855, the Rev. Dr. Bellows, pastor.*

The writings of Linsley, of Priestley, of Belsham, of Wakefield, were not wholly unfamiliar works in this city; nor could those early fathers, so often ransacked in the polemical disquisitions on the church of the first three centuries, have been altogether over-

* The Rev. Dr. Osgood, in his Historical Discourse, entitled "Twenty-five Years of a Congregation," thus expresses himself, when speaking of the origin and progress of the Unitarian worship in this city:—"Dr. Channing preached to a large audience in the Hall of the Medical College, Barclay street, which was granted by the Trustees, notwithstanding violent opposition from some of the professors of the institution. Thus, to the medical profession belongs the honor of giving our form of Liberal Christianity the first public hearing in New York."

looked by our scholars and divines. This inference I deduce from the indignation which so generally sprung up among the patrons of the work when the American edition of Rees' Cyclopædia was commenced by Samuel F. Bradford. This enterprising publisher had in his prospectus announced that that great undertaking would be revised, corrected, enlarged, and adapted to this country. It was soon seen that, among other articles, that of accommodation in theology, which the learned Rees affirmed was a method that served as a way for solving some of the greatest difficulties relating to the prophecies, had been maltreated by an American reviser, reputed to be Dr. Ashbel Green, in Bradford's reprint. This unwarrantable act created uneasiness here, as well as among our eastern brethren, and had nearly jeopardized the patriotic intentions of the noble-hearted Philadelphian, Bradford, whose purpose was to enrich the literature and philosophy of our Republic with that monumental work. The dissatisfaction at this literary fraud pervaded so many patrons here and elsewhere that I, even at that early date, came to the conclusion that Unitarianism could scarcely be classed among the novelties of the day, and was not limited to any one section of the country. The perverted article doubtless partook originally of the religious faith of the London editor. Never did the old Anthology Club present a nobler independence on the rights of opinion and of literary property than in their criticism on the affected emendation of the American copy of Rees. It is but justice to state of this great work, which still so justly holds a place in our libraries, that these disgraceful mutilations of Rees ceased after the reprint of the first volume of the Cyclopædia, and the honest Bradford had weighty reasons to congratulate himself on the seasonable reproofs administered against the unjust editors by the Tudors, and Kirklands, and Buckminsters of "The Literary Emporium."

While in London I was a frequent visitor of Dr. Rees. A more captivating example of the Christian charities enshrined in one mortal, the eye could not light on. He possessed a tall and athletic frame, and a countenance of great benignity. He had all the requisites of a powerful preacher, in person, in manner, in tone, and in diction. His urbanity and his placidity of disposition secured the esteem of all who approached him. He told me that his labors were then nearly brought to a close; that for more than thirty years he had been confined to his study, an ordinary room; that his diurnal labor was of many hours; that, save his Sabbath preaching at the Old Jewry, his only exercise had been his limited walk daily to his publishers, the Longmans. His fair and lively skin, his bright eye and his wholesome appearance, with such a life of mental devotion and such confinement, put at nought all my theoretical doctrines on the laws of health. He must have been more than a teetotaller. I was informed he was the last of the Doddridge wig order, an imposing article, but which yielded in dimensions and artistic elaboration to the more formidable one which invested the brain-case of the great hellenist, Dr. Samuel Parr, with its distensive and seemingly patulous gyrations. To the curious in habiliments, I may add, that the wig of that right worthy, lately with us, Dr. Livingston, was of the Doddridge order, that of old Dr. Rodgers, Samuel Parr's. Nor is it trifling to state the fact, for there was a time, according to Southey, when the wig was considered as necessary for a learned head, as an ivy bush for an owl. You will pardon this digression on Rees' Cyclopædia, inasmuch as it elucidates the point I would sustain, were this a fit occasion, that in the origin and spread of the Unitarian creed in this country, we are hardly justified to limit our attention to the movements of our Boston or Eastern friends. The well-known letter of Franklin to Stiles supports this view, and we have seen that when occasion has prompted, its advocates rise up limited to no special locality. The community that can enumerate among its supporters such writers and scholars as Channing, Dewey, Osgood, and Bellows, need cherish no apprehension that their cause will fall through from a stultified indifference. But I find myself launching in deep waters, and will near the shore.

Enough and more than enough has been said of the workings of the principles of religious toleration among us; they furnish instructive proofs of the freedom secured to the people by our admirable constitutional form of government; the intellect knows it, the searcher after truth is sustained by it.

With a very brief notice of the Episcopalian denomination, I shall terminate these hasty sketches of religious matters. The Episcopalians of this metropolis have exercised a great influence on the interests of learning among New Yorkers, and on their institutions of public instruction and humanity. They have also proved warm friends to the New York Historical Society.

The disruption of the colonies from the Mother Country proved more disastrous in its immediate effects to the Protestant Episcopal Church than to that perhaps of any other religious association. The ties which bound her to the forms and ceremonials of the Church of England, were strong and numerous; her ministers, with few exceptions, favored the cause of the loyalists, and consequently in a large majority of instances were, upon the restoration of peace, compelled to abandon their pastoral charges, and seek a livelihood elsewhere. This consequence, with the disasters of the times, resulted in a deserted ministry and in a disabled and poverty-stricken religious community. The conscientious Churchman, bewailing the state of affairs and anxious of the future, looked forward with fluctuating hopes to the period when a happy issue might be found in the various deliberations which now occupied the minds of the friends of the Episcopate, not unlike those which agitated the patriots of the Revolution amidst their discussions on the adoption of the Articles of Confederation by the old Congress. At length a Convention was held in Philadelphia, which continued from the 27th of September to the 7th of October, 1785, and delegates appeared from New York, New Jersey, Pennsylvania, Delaware, Maryland, Virginia, and South Carolina. Its labors brought forth the Protestant Episcopal Book of Common Prayer, proposed for the Protestant Episcopal Church, printed by Hall and Sellers, in 1786. This book, now rarely to be found, received the name of the Proposed Book. It was reprinted at London in 1787; it contained no Nicene Creed, nor Athanasian Creed; it had the Apostolic Creed, but omitted "he descended into hell." It had a special prayer for the then existing government. It had a special supplication in the liturgy for the then Congress, and a form of service or prayer for the 4th of July.

The Convention was again held in Philadelphia, in September, 1789, William White, President, for the purpose of settling Articles of Union, discipline, uniformity of worship, and general government among all the churches in the United States. The Prayer Book was now so adjusted as to meet with great acceptance and with full approval. At the instance of the English bishops, the passage "he descended into hell," was restored, with a proviso, that the words "he went into the place of departed spirits," might or might not be substituted. The Nicene Creed was restored; the prayers were made to conform to the now established government, for the President and all in civil authority. This Convention agreed to abolish the service for the 4th of July, but allowed each bishop the power of providing a suitable service for that and all other political occasions. In 1792, Bishop Provoost, who had been absent from indisposition at the former Convention, presided. The Church ordinal, for the ordination of deacons and priests, and the consecration of bishops, was agreed upon. It was printed by Hugh Gaine, in 1793. The articles of religion were agreed to in Convention in 1801, and have since that time been published with the Book of Common Prayer.

This brief notice of the history of the Book of Common Prayer, according to the use of the Protestant Episcopal Church in the United States of America, seemed necessary, inasmuch as that highly prized volume is the recognized standard of the Episcopal Church of this country. It has proved of inestimable importance to the progress of the Church, as the bond of union of that important religious community; it has preserved intact her forms and ceremonials, and her devotions; it has saved her from division and disunion; it has suppressed intestine broils; it has promoted uniformity of worship, a most important object; and by it she has avoided the distractions and the local strifes which have too often disturbed the harmony and fellowship of other Christian associations. If from the cold lips and still colder hearts of the mere formalist, its reading has sometimes wanted the spirit of prayer, how much oftener has it saved from vulgar importunities in prayer, and rescued the finer emotions of the soul from irreverent demands of Heaven, and noxious crudities. It turns with conscious rectitude from the incoherent ravings of enthusiasm, and disdains to look on the elongated visage of a scaramouch. The north and the south, the east and the west, hold it in equal reverence, and do homage to its unparalleled beauty of diction and its devotional sentiment. Living or dying, it yields the bread of life.

New York had her share in that goodly work; her learned Provoost was a member of both Conventions that framed it, and the first consecration in the Church of an additional bishop, was the act of Episcopacy by Provoost, in this city, in the laying on of hands on Thomas John Claggett, D.D., of Maryland, in September, 1792, at which ceremonial White, of Pennsylvania, Madison, of Virginia, and Seabury, of Connecticut, assisted. Provoost, White, and Madison, were the regularly consecrated bishops of the English Episcopate, of the American Episcopal Church, the two former having been elevated to the Episcopate by Moore, Archbishop of Canterbury, in the chapel of Lambeth

Palace, in 1787, and Madison in 1790, in the same place, by the same authority. Bishop Seabury had received consecration in 1784, at Aberdeen, Scotland, by three nonjuring bishops, and by this convenient action of the bishops of the English consecration, and of Bishop Seabury, the American Episcopal Church (as it is believed intentionally) united both Episcopates in theirs, thereby closing the door against the future occurrence of questions which might prove delicate and embarrassing. Seabury was a man of strong native powers, of cultivated intellect, of extensive influence, ardent in the cause of Episcopacy. The Church may with sincerity ever hold him in grateful remembrance. When her sorrows were gravest, he imparted consolation; when her weakness was greatest, he yielded her strength. Her tribulations only added to his zealous efforts in her behalf. He adhered to the royal side in the great contest with the Mother Country, and dwelt among the refugees in New York. He united in the protest declaring abhorrence of all unlawful congresses and committees, and doubtless with conscientious views, under the patronage of the obnoxious Tryon, delivered a discourse to fear God and honor the king. He died a pensioner of the British government, and I incline to the opinion, was looked upon somewhat with a jaundiced vision by those devoted patriots, Provoost and White.

It has been more than once affirmed, and the declaration is in print, that Bishop Provoost, as senior presbyter, and senior in the ministry, was consecrated first, and Bishop White next, though in the same day and hour, February 4, 1787. The son-in-law of Provoost, C. D. Colden, a man of veracity, assured me such was the case. If so, Provoost is to be recorded as the Father of the American Episcopate. It is painful to pluck a hair from the venerable head of the apostolic White, but we are dealing with history. White, who died at the advanced age of eighty-nine years, lived to see the American Church with some twenty-three bishops, he having officiated at nearly every consecration. What vast obligations are due to his hallowed memory by the American Episcopate for the wise counsels, the many and inestimable services of that divine character!

Dissent, however lowly, Episcopacy, however high, will coalesce in opinion of the varied knowledge and classical attainments of Provoost, the piety and beneficence of Moore, and the talents, zeal, and ceaseless activity of Hobart. These eminent dignitaries of the church may, for their several qualities, be ranked among the most conspicuous of their order, who have flourished in New York; and were it practicable, we would fain dwell in particular upon the earnestness and achievements of the last-named. His death is too recent to require much at our hands; sorrow at his early departure was universal; it was felt as an irreparable loss to the interests of a great community, who had almost by his individual efforts been extricated from many difficulties and risen to a commanding importance in numbers and influence. The aptitude of Hobart, in the work of the ministry, and his astonishing executive talent, have scarcely a parallel: his vigilance noticed every thing that tended either to retard the advancement or quicken the progress of the Episcopal Church. He was desirous of a learned priesthood, and much of his time and his intellect were given to the maintenance of the General Theological Seminary; he was ardent for the practical, and sought befitting laborers, as the harvest was truly great. Many of the Episcopate had a richer fund of classical erudition; but not one could be pointed out who possessed an industry and devotion superior to his. It may be questioned whether he lost an idle hour during his whole career as bishop for nearly twenty years. He exercised a weighty influence on public sentiment, and the purity of his life stamped his opinions with a corresponding value. The Church to him was all in all. His adhesion to what he deemed its orthodoxy, allowed of no deviation from its prescriptions, nor could he cherish reconciliation with the doubting and the latitudinarian. His frankness enabled his opponents always to know where to find him; from his decision of character, he could hardly be expected to live in perfect charity with all men. He was more than once absorbed in controversies on ecclesiastical polity, and his sentiments rendered him obnoxious to a portion of his diocese. The harshest opinion I ever heard him utter was, that Heber was only a ballad writer. The sentiment must have taken possession of his bosom from the circumstance that the Bishop of Calcutta gave countenance to the British Bible Society; and not a few of Bishop Hobart's friends regretted the pertinacity with which he opposed the organization of a like institution here. Like Herbert Marsh, he dreaded the consequences of distributing the Scriptures without the Book of Common Prayer. The lamented Milner, whom the Church still mourns, did not wholly escape the penalty of resistance to the views of the American prelate, and that eminent statesman and patriot, Rufus

King, after having been chosen a Vice President of that National Society, resigned his office and withdrew from his high station at the special solicitation of his personal friend, Bishop Hobart. In his conversation, the Bishop was animated, abounding in anecdotes and general knowledge, and was particularly attractive. His temper was sprightly; he avowed his opinions with great freedom. He had strong feelings in behalf of American institutions, and was averse to the union of church and state affairs. The sincerity of his Christian belief was edifyingly demonstrated in the manner of his death. He sickened of bilious disease while on his diocesan visitation, at Auburn; on the morning of his final departure, the early sun shone in upon his chamber; "it is the last time," said he, "that I shall witness the rising sun; I shall soon behold the Sun of righteousness." Thus died a great and good man. He who would know more of this eminent pillar of the Church, will consult the Life, written by the venerable rector of Trinity, Dr. Berrian, the Records published by Professor M'Vickar, and the Memorial by the Rev. Dr. Schroeder.

Before I conclude this portion of my subject, I must be permitted to say a few words on the literature of the Church; and I am happy to add, that New York has not been behindhand with her sister States in her contributions towards that great object. I have already adverted to the low and precarious condition of Episcopacy at and about the time when the Constitution of the American government was brought into practical action, and the many difficulties which encompassed the Church in the scattered and limited number of her ministry. The noble and venerable Society for propagating the Gospel in foreign parts, had indeed sown precious seeds in divers places over the land. But the Church was prostrate, involved in fiscal troubles, and wanting in those effective measures of enlightenment indispensably requisite to rear up her intellectual greatness. Every intelligent individual is ready to acknowledge, with cheerful feelings, that we owe to our brethren of other denominations a large debt for the many able and instructive works with which they have enriched the theological literature of the nation. We are aware of the scholarship of Andover, the biblical expositions of Princeton, and the graces of classical composition which have proceeded from old Harvard and Yale. In days past we remember Edwards, and Emerson, and Stiles, and Dwight. We forget not Hodge, Robinson, Park, Norton, Stewart, Mason, and a host of others; and we believe there is substantial reason for the high estimation in which the works of many American divines are held, arising from the intrinsic excellence of their respective authorship; and if report deceive us not, we have the assurance that among the most successful reprints abroad, are what we shall please to call American theology.

As respects the literature of the Episcopal Church, it seems to be most noteworthy for its conservative element. It is preceded by the Prayer Book, or is in close fraternity with it, and this book of sacred wisdom gives a complexion to the thoughts and workings of the ministry of the Church that stamps a peculiarity more or less legible on its intellectual progeny. Like the pendulum in clockwork, it controls its movements, guards against irregularity, and secures harmony in all its parts. We thence see that its elaborations are characterized less by diversity of speculation and startling novelties, and is to be noticed more for exegetical exposition and the elucidation of scriptural truth. Both by the pulpit and by the pen it is disposed more to persuade than to threaten, more to lead than to drive; and finds it more consonant to its own emotions to announce the glad tidings from lips of praise, than in wrathful accents proclaim a Redeemer's love. Such it may be affirmed is the policy of the Church, and such is the attribute of her literature. Principles such as are now indicated, pervade all her writings, and if so be an anathema is sometimes found, it is to be considered as an exception to her whole policy. The divinity which holds possession in her breast, is the redeeming power of gospel truth. What triumphs she has secured by such procedure will be best learned by comparing her vast increase and united strength at this present time with her feeble condition and disjointed state at her first organization. Let her in conscious purity and in the plenitude of divine grace cherish the most confident hopes. Let her go on her way rejoicing. Let her be ever jealous of her high title, the Protestant Episcopal Church. Ever let the noble army of reformers command her admiration and her loudest plaudits. If the ignorant comprehend not her simplicity, and the cynical complain that her covenant has been invaded in these latter days by effete devices, let them be told all is as a passing cloud, pregnant with untold riches, and that her brightness, thanks to a good Providence, is hourly becoming more clear and beautiful, and her foundation stronger and stronger on the Rock of Ages. Let schismatics know that exploded theories find no aliment within her bosom, that obsolete formularies are at war with her doctrines and her discipline. She repudiates a pantomimic worship. Her formulary is the conformity of the heart to the plain and simple and comprehensible doctrines of apostolic communication. Let her feel that she has arrived to that vigor by inherent strength, that in confidence she may trust in her manhood and go forth triumphant. What has served her so well for more than half a century, will suffice much longer. Her hardest trials have passed, and she is neither debilitated nor impure. The sound need no crutch. All that she now asks is, to live in harmony with the professing Christians of every sect and denomination. She is ready, she is willing, she trusts she is able, to do the work of her Master, and whether under the humble roof of the village chapel, or within the dome of the mighty cathedral, she has learned by experience that her coin will pass current without amalgamation.

A word or two on the literature of the Church. If the army of New England divines has almost overwhelmed the land with their achievements in the field of literature and theology, there is still room enough left for us to point out a few landmarks secured by the professors of the Episcopal Church. She has scattered abroad in profusion single discourses of elevated thought, strong devotional sentiments, and sound practical edification. True she lacks earnestness in historical detail, and seems too listless of the character and services of her predecessors. She ought, in an especial manner, no longer to overlook the vast importance of her history, faithfully written, for the honor of her devoted sons, and for the study and improvement of her future disciples; at this present time, too, when the materials are still accessible, it behooves her to gather together the incidents of her career amid untold trials, and offer them, in a becoming form, as a demonstration of her devotion and wisdom in her high commission. It is gratifying to see that within a few years past the subject has, among all her calls of duty, awakened desires in some of the most efficient of her people to remove the obloquy which has too long rested on her, and several able writers have recently come to the rescue. The "Memoirs of the Protestant Episcopal Church," published years ago by the venerable White, have been followed by those of the Church of South Carolina, by Dr. Dalcho; by the Contributions of Dr. Hawks, in illustration of the Churches of Virginia and of Maryland; by the History of Trinity Church, New York, by Dr. Berrian; by the Continuity of the Church of England, by Dr. Seabury; by the History of Dr. Dorr; by two volumes of a newly formed association, the Protestant Episcopal Historical Society, having its origin, I believe, in this city; and, very lately, by a work of curious incidents, the History of St. John's Church, Elizabethtown, New Jersey. Some years since we had also historical materials of ecclesiastical value, in the Centennial Discourse concerning the Church at Quincy, by Dr. Cutler. All this argues well. Bishop Mead's Reminiscences are materials of instructive import; and the Reminiscences of Bishop Chase will long hold in esteem the character and the arduous labors of the Pioneer Bishop of the West. That hardy and indomitable man has left the workings of a strong spirit in behalf of a mighty cause. He was the architect of his own renown; he had little book learning, but much knowledge of men. Having early laid plans for his professional life, no obstacles intimidated him; and his determination, the result of his own cogitations, never forsook him. His settled purpose was for others, not for himself; he could therefore present a bolder front in his pressing demands for the accomplishment of his great designs. His track through almost unknown wilds will be studied hereafter with a more appreciating judgment, and the blessings he has bestowed on the Church find a record from the pen that records national benefits, deduced from his fruitful doings. Many of his journeyings were through a portion of that country, then so little understood, which the brave Carver had travelled; and one may also place in juxtaposition these two intrepid men, Jonathan and Philander; the *sic vos non vobis* being equally the temporal reward of both.

As associated with the Church's History, is the Memoirs of her eminent men; and we are not to complain either of lack of numbers or of value in those already published. The biography of Samuel Johnson, the first President of Columbia College, by Chandler, is the most engaging of this department of literary labor; and we cannot regret too much that so few of the great mass of papers from which this volume was made up have found a place in this admirable work. The Memoirs of White are next in order of time, and are indispensable to the ecclesiastical historian; while those of Hobart, Griswold, Moore, Ravenscroft, Bedell and Wharton, unfold characteristics valuable in elucidation of Church matters. It is not, however, to be concealed, that, like many religious biographies, whether by authors abroad or at home, they often lack interest from the absence of personal detail, and of that enlivening spirit which gives to biography its most engaging attraction.

Honorable mention deserves to be made of the learned labor of Dr. Samuel Farmer Jarvis. This ripe scholar had been professor of biblical history in the recently organized General Theological Seminary of the Protestant Episcopal Church, and was subsequently made Historiographer of the Church at large by the General Convention. In his Ecclesiastical Chronology and History he evinced the greatest research and devotion. Like notice is due to the various writings of Bishop Hopkins of Vermont; and it is gratifying to see the reception his last work has met with by the reading public,—I mean his American Citizen. The devoted Episcopalian might often look with satisfaction into the writings of Bishops Hobart, Brownell, Potter, Whittingham, Eastburn, Burgess, M'Ilvaine, Onderdonk, and Doane, and find proofs of scholastic lore in the pages of Verplanck, Winslow, Coit, Griffin and Spencer.

The canons of the Church have been elucidated by Judge Murray Hoffman of the New York bar, and by the Rev. Dr. Hawks. The Constitution and Canons, by the latter, was a peculiarly appropriate subject for her ecclesiastical historian, and the competent have given their testimony in behalf of the excellence of the undertaking. I shall conclude these very brief and imperfect sketches of the literary labors of the Church with a name widely known and appreciated by the erudite of both hemispheres, Samuel H. Turner. Dr. Turner's reputation for varied and profound scholarship, for rabbinical knowledge, and the activity of his pen in critical expositions of sacred writ, have secured him permanent renown. I am forbidden an enumeration of his many works. The Theological Seminary, in which he has labored so long, may congratulate herself on the honors with which such a professor enriches her, and freely add his name to the select list of her ablest associates. Proofs sufficient, I think, have already been advanced to show that the literature of the Church is not locked up in sealed libraries, but is an active power; and from her present advanced and improved state, we may draw an equally safe inference that her religion lies not dormant in the heart, but is an absolute principle, industrious in the work of faith.

I leave ecclesiastical affairs, and propose saying a few words on a subject which the philosopher may pronounce of equal importance in a national point of view,—I allude to our system of public education. It has become a vast subject in this our day, and commands the admiration of remote nations. The faithful historian of our first settlers, Mr. Brodhead, in his minute research, has dwelt upon the theme with the genuine spirit of the philanthropist, and clearly pointed out with what earnestness the sagacity of the Dutch penetrated into the wisdom of establishments for that purpose; and so early as 1633, only twenty-four years after the arrival of Hudson, organized the first school in New Amsterdam. "Neither the perils of war," says Brodhead, "nor the busy pursuits of gain, nor the excitement of political strife, ever caused them to neglect the duty of educating their offspring." And with a love of the past, he has recorded the name of this first schoolmaster, Adam Rœlandsen; and it well merits to be further stated, that Rœlandsen's original establishment continues in a prosperous condition to this day, and is the parochial school of the Protestant Reformed Dutch Church, supported by voluntary contributions. I have some recollection of the first formation of that system in this city, which finally eventuated in the system of public schools. Only one year after your first measures were adopted to establish the Historical Society did the duty of enlarging the domain of knowledge by public instruction take possession of our city rulers. The Trinity Church charity school, and other free schools under the governance of different religious associations, had indeed for years an existence, and were more or less prosperous; but the great mass of children belonging to parents of no religious order were sadly neglected, save those who could accomplish the means of enlightenment at private institutions. The names of that noble band of citizens who were the applicants for an act to establish a free school in the city of New York for the education of such poor children as do not belong to, or are not provided for by any religious society, are duly recorded in the reports of the Board of Education; and he who looks over the list will recognize that many of the names of our prominent residents, of exalted excellence, are found in the number. Under its restricted powers, the society organized its first school in May, 1806, with forty scholars. With enlarged charter powers, aided by the liberality of the city government, in 1808 they were provided a spacious building, which admitted five hundred pupils.

I remember well the discourse delivered at the

opening of this improved edifice, at the corner of Tryon Row and Chatham street, by De Witt Clinton, the moving spirit of the whole affair. He was the president of the society, and the Board of Education, in their Report of 1854, say well when they announce that the address was worthy of the occasion, "as sowing the seed wheat of all harvests of education which subsequent years have gathered into our garners." I have accompanied Mr. Clinton in those earlier days, in his tour of inspection, with Thomas Eddy, Jacob Morton, Samuel Wood, Joseph Curtis, Robert Bowne, Charles Wilkes, Cadwallader D. Colden, and others, and I can testify to the scrutinizing devotion which Mr. Clinton gave to every thing that seemed calculated for the promotion of the great and novel design. By the death of Mr. Curtis very recently, all, I believe, of that philanthropic corps are departed. I see none left of the original body of incorporators.

It is impossible at this time to be more minute or dwell longer on this grateful subject. In every condition of public trust to which Clinton was chosen through life, he never forgot education and the public schools. Every message of his, while governor, descants on the vast theme, and his suggestions, years ago, as head of the State, may, I think, be honestly stated to have led to that special department, the Normal Schools. He is the first individual I ever heard descant on their immense importance to the proper rearing of competent tutors, and on the provision which ought to be made for such an undertaking. I can scarcely conceive of a greater subject for a public discourse than the origin, the progress, and present state of our system of Public Education; in every condition, from its humble beginning up to its commanding importance at the present day, from the Free School Society of 1805 through the change to the Public School Society of 1826, providing for all classes of children; next the Ward school organization of the then called District schools; then to its present consolidation under the Board of Education of the City of New York, a period of nearly half a century. Well may that enlightened citizen and public-spirited character, E. C. Benedict, in his Report of 1854, as president, say, "The services of those philanthropic laborers in the noblest of causes has imposed upon the city a debt of gratitude that can never be fitly estimated, much less repaid." During that period it has conferred the blessings of instruction on 600,000 children, and on more than 12,000 teachers. So long as the influence of those children and their teachers shall be felt, (and when will it cease?) so long, justly adds Mr. Benedict, "shall the usefulness of the Public School Society continue." I will add, that according to the last Report of the Board of Education from the present enlightened President, Wm. H. Neilson, the whole number of schools within its jurisdiction during the year 1855, was 271. The glory and imperishable excellence of our public system of education, enhanced by the influence of our self-government, by universal freedom and a free press, were demonstrated to be in accordance with enlightened public intelligence, when at the election of 1850 the free school question was submitted to the popular suffrage. Free schools were sustained in this city by a vote of 39,075 to 1,011, a majority of nearly 40 to 1. If more were wanting in confirmation, how easily could we swell the testimony by the recorded opinions in behalf of the vast and enduring benefits of knowledge among the masses by the testimony of our wisest statesmen and patriots. And let us ever keep before us the vital principle that the colossal proportions of the republic are endowed by education alone with a proportionate cohesive power. Where education moreover is popular, the creative faculty abounds; and it is characteristic of such a state, that the people thus blessed daily achieve some new step in advance, whether it be in the modification of a rail or in new powers for the steam-engine.

The Free Academy, which, it has been very properly remarked, gives completeness to the system of public instruction, and is an integrant branch of the whole system for the enlightenment of the people, possesses the great advantage of a liberal system of education similar to that which is embraced in our colleges for the highest departments of study. Indeed, few, if any, of our collegiate establishments hold out so ample a course of instruction in classical literature, in modern languages, in mathematical and physical science. The existence of the Academy is brief, yet already have precious fruits been scattered broad-cast over the land, to the wonder and admiration of the most appreciating minds. I, unfortunately for myself, am but in a limited degree acquainted with the professors of that great school; but if Dr. Gibbs is to be taken as a specimen of its teachers, unbounded confidence may be reposed in the acquisitions of its scholars. I only repeat what is uttered daily, that the distinguished principal, Dr. Webster, has solved the problem, how manifold are the benefits which may flow from a wise administration of able collegiate authority.

Let me in all sincerity ask, in what other place may the poorest and the humblest child of indigence find instruction from the A, B, C, to the highest branches of classical and scientific knowledge, through every stage of his study, without one dollar's expense to the recipient; and all this, every device and measure, planned and accomplished since our organization in 1804. Let all praise be given to our constituted authorities for this exemplar of their wisdom and patriotic forethought: let above all others that capacious mind which is alike seen in the union of the Erie and the Hudson and in our noble system of education, become the theme of collegiate eloquence and historical record. Let our children and their children's children keep within memory the names of Hawley, Bernard, Randall, and Benedict. But this request is perhaps superfluous; the bounty is ever before us, the givers cannot be forgotten. To those alive to local history and the origin of great practical ideas, says the accomplished essayist Tuckerman, in his biographical volume, daily observation keeps fresh the memory of Clinton.*

* Most astounding disclosures were made at the London Educational Conference in June last, 1856, on the great question, the enlightenment of the people. I extract from the report, which appeared in the Illustrated London News: "Notwithstanding all the voluntary efforts, all the benevolence, all the liberality of Churchmen and of Dissenters, of corporations and of individuals, there are in England and Wales, out of nearly five millions of children between the ages of three and fifteen years, little more than two millions who attend any school whatever, leaving 2,861,848 —nearly three millions—who are not in the receipt of school instruction." "Nor is even this state of things, bad as it is, the worst part of the case. Of the two millions of children who attend existing schools, we are informed by the Prince that only six hundred thousand—less than one-third —are above the age of nine. In other words, more than one-half of the poor children of England receive no school instruction at all, and two-

The transition is not altogether violent, in leaving one species of instruction for another—in dismissing the system of school education and taking up the Stage, so long reckoned a source of useful knowledge, and by many still deemed capable of becoming an enlightened monitor. But with the drama, as with many other subjects that properly belong to a discourse accommodated to this occasion, I am subjected to a painful brevity; for what adequate notions can be imparted within the few moments at command, of the dramatic occurrences of New York during the past fifty years? It has so happened that for forty years of my life I have been, with slight intermissions, the medical adviser and physician of many of the leading heroes of the sock and buskin, from the arrival of the great George Frederick Cooke in 1810, to the departure of the classical Macready in 1849; and I am apprehensive that of all the individuals commemorated in Dunlap's Biography of Cooke, I am perhaps the sole survivor.

I cannot say that I have ever been stage-struck or dramatically mad in my admiration of the histrionic profession; yet as one ever gratified with the displays of intellectual power, I have experienced the raptures inspired by genius, in a vocation which, while it holds the mirror up to nature, is the acknowledged school of oratory, and has received in all ages among the refined, the countenance and support of many of the loftiest

thirds of the remainder are taken away from school at an age so early that it is quite impossible for them to have received any enduring benefit from school teaching. The result is, if these figures are correct, that only one child out of every eight in this rich, civilized, and Christian country, remains at school after its ninth year."

minds and most sympathizing hearts. Moreover, I think it not too much to say, that my professional intercourse with actors has enabled me to obtain a view of dramatic character and of dramatic life, which could scarcely be expected to fall within the scope of the mere beholder of scenic representation, who never perhaps had passed behind the foot-lights, or been familiar with that condition of physical and mental toil which the ceremonies and performances due to "personation," impose on the feelings of the successful artist.

I take it for granted that no intelligent man will hold in doubt the fact, that the life of the player is one of severe trial, of great demands on the physical powers, of incessant mental anxiety, and of precarious rewards. Yet have I known many members of that calling filled with the largest benevolence and enriched with the graces which dignify human nature. The actor's life is especially subjected to the caprices of fortune; the platform on which he stands is ever uncertain; as a general truth he encounters adversity with more than ordinary fortitude. I have known many instances of this nature; the mimic world has its stern realities not less than the actual, and the wardrobe no more protects its denizen than do the common habiliments of the ordinary citizen. "The life of an actor," says a modern essayist of the school of English undefiled, "is a severe trial of humanity. His temptations are many; his fortitude, too, often ineffectual; his success precarious. If he be resolute, uncontaminated by the society of his associates, and a genuine artist besides, he is worthy not only the praise of the moralist, but also deserving the admiration of the critic. The prejudice against the profession, like most prevailing prejudices, is founded on general truth; but it is frequently absurd and baseless."* If the stage has fallen from its high estate, and failed to raise the genius and to mend the heart, to elevate the moral sentiment by heroic action and sublime example, let not its sad decline rest solel ywith the representatives of Shakspeare and Jonson; let something be ascribed to the revolutions of taste and to the mutability of popular opinion; but more than all, let us suffer within ourselves the chagrin of self-condemnation, like the dyspeptic patient, who in searching for the causes of his own horrors, finds them to have originated from the pernicious aliment in which his disturbed propensities had led him most unwittingly to indulge. "The love of the drama," says the poet Campbell, "is a public instinct, that requires to be regulated, but is too deep for eradication. I am no such bigot for the stage," continues he, "as to say that it is necessarily a school of morals; for, by bad management, it may be made the reverse; and I think, on the whole, that the drama rather follows than leads public morals." The drama is legitimately the school of human life; it has vast accommodations, but its origin is in the human heart; in its nature it is the concentration and the exposition of the passions and the doings of man. Let it cherish fidelity to its great trust; let it so conduct itself as not to fall below the intelligence of its arbitrators; never forgetting that the schoolmaster is abroad. The remedy is within grasp; and its restoration is not altogether a thing of fancy.

* Characters and Criticisms, by W. Alfred Jones, A. M., New York, Vol. 2, p. 182. 12mo. 1857.

The scholar, however fastidious, cannot wholly disregard a theme which found favor among the lucubrations of the mighty Warburton: he who would penetrate into the ethics of human life need not suffer apprehension of evil from studies which absorbed many of the precious hours of the great moralist, Johnson; nor can the Christian philosopher be afraid to reason on the subject with the example before him of Young, the successful author of the Revenge, and the poet of the Night Thoughts, a work whose devotional excellence has made it a manual of closest study to millions of human souls, wherever revealed truth has been recognized.

I am not so confident as to presume that what I may utter can have any influence on a New York community, either on the fortunes or destiny of the stage. It has been decried by the best of men, and it has been countenanced by the wisest. It was formerly supported by religious partialities, and every body is aware that it owes its origin to religion, and that the first actors were priests or missionaries. An illiterate multitude were thus enlightened, and the clergy with an inherent sagacity represented the wonders of belief and the actions of the gods in appropriate temples. For a long while it was a school of instruction, and for manners and behavior, and on this account the stage is still higher to be appreciated. Shakspeare has taught more history to the masses than all the schoolmasters, from the time when the first pedagogue was installed, and Lord Chesterfield's dicta have proved a mere cipher compared to the operations which scenic influence has wrought in mollifying the intercourse of society. Yet there is a progress in refinement which eclipses the exhibition of the stage, and he whose mind is stored with much knowledge, will abandon theatricals as having lost their former interest with him. It certainly is a foe to hypocrisy, and that alone, with the real philanthropist, is no small recommendation. It proves a wondrous relief to the laborious man and the worn intellect, and is a happy succedaneum for diversions less beneficial to good morals and good health. Grant that the sphere of the stage is indeed local and its displays fugacious, yet it leaves a lasting impression on the human heart. Its rich literature bears the impress of genius and cannot be overlooked by the accomplished scholar. But I must break off here. Let those who would raise an indiscriminate outcry against the stage, read the calm and dispassionate Address of Dr. Bellows, lately delivered in the Academy of Music, before the Dramatic Fund Association.

The history of the first introduction of the stage in the American colonies is full of perplexity. Dunlap, our leading dramatic historian, in his work on the American Theatre, a performance of acknowledged merit, has blended his facts with so many errors, that we strive in vain to derive from his pages a true knowledge of the subject. He was doubtless led into most of his difficulties by too great reliance on the story given by Burk, in his History of Virginia. I have endeavored to make the case clearer, and have sought out curious facts in Parker's News Boy. The introduction of the drama in the American colonies was in this city, on Monday evening, the 26th of February 1750, in a convenient room for the purpose, in one of the buildings which had belonged to the estate of Rip Van

Dam (a renowned Knickerbocker) in Nassau street. The play was the historical tragedy of Richard the Third, written originally by Shakspeare, and altered by Colley Cibber, under the management of Lewis Hallam, whose family consisted of his wife, a son Lewis, and a younger son, Adam, with a niece, Miss Hallam. His elder son, Lewis, was but twelve years of age. Dunlap says, that he made his first appear. ance in September, 1752, at Williamsburg, in Virginia. The younger, Adam, appeared in October, 1753, in this city, in the character of "Tom Thumb." He had a daughter, who became Mrs. Mattocks in England. It may be that this company, under manager Hallam, appeared next in Williamsburg; but on the 15th of April, 1754, they opened in Philadelphia with the "Fair Penitent."

We have not before us the cast of the play (Richard the Third) enacted in this city. It possesses so many *dramatis personæ*, that we have little doubt that several of the company had to take double parts. Rigby, we may safely infer, enacted Richard Third. There was no accommodation of boxes, only pit and gallery. There was no farce after Richard Third. The permission for the performance was given by the British governor, Clinton. Lewis Hallam, at the age of twenty-nine, appeared in Lord Ogleby, the year after the comedy was written, in 1767. This part he played for forty years; the last time in the Park theatre, in 1807, and witnesses of this fact still survive. Manager Hallam died in Philadelphia in 1808. This company was generally designated by the name of the Old American Company, and Hallam the father of the American stage.

Thus it appears that this city has enjoyed the drama for upwards of one hundred years. Of that fifty which had passed away before the establishment of our Historical Society, I intend not now to enlarge. Suffice it to say, as to the character and abilities of the performers of the American company our oldest playgoers were often heard to speak in terms of highest approbation; and when we enumerate Hallam, Henry, Harwood, Jefferson, Cooper, Fennell, Johnstone, Hodgkinson and his wife, Mrs. Oldmixon, and Mrs. Merry, we need not apprehend that their plaudits were unmerited. The names of several of these efficient actors of the olden times may be seen recorded on the bills which announced the arrival of Cooke.

To one who contemplates the progress of art and education in our land, it will at once occur that with theatricals, as with instruction generally, we depended almost altogether upon supplies from abroad. Our preachers, our professors in colleges, our artists, our books were rarely indigenous, and the stage illustrates our early reliance on the mother country in an equal, if not in a greater degree, than in any of the other vocations of busy life. If our condition was once so restricted that farmer Giles imported from beyond the seas wooden axe-handles when the country was overrun with forests, surely it may be pronounced to have been admissible that a truthful Cordelia might be included among importable articles, for the praiseworthy design of disciplining the humanities of the man of refinement. At the time of the first representation of Richard the Third, animadversions appeared on the corruptions of the stage; but, in its defence, Whitfield is cited in its behalf, inasmuch as he had ascribed his inimitable gesture and bewitching address to his having acted in his youth; and the writer moreover adds, with great earnestness, that the abuse of a thing against its use is no argument, as there is nothing in this world but must fall before such demolishing kind of logic. There was little dramatic criticism, however, among us in the early days of the theatre.

The chronicler who would be faithful to the history of the stage in New York would be compelled to say something concerning that period which elapsed between the commencement of the great American war of 1776 and its end in 1783. During that interval the English plays of Garrick, Foote, Cumberland, Coleman, O'Keefe, Sheridan, and others, reached from time to time this country, and were enacted by the officers of the army and navy, and by select aids in private or social circles; and a remarkable peculiarity of the times seems to have been, that it was quite a common circumstance to appropriate or designate some leading or prominent individual among the inhabitants of the city as the character drawn by the dramatist abroad. *Qui capit, ille facit.* Thus, when the Busy Body appeared, it was thought that Dr. Atwood would be the best exemplar of it. Atwood, as all who hear me probably know, was the first practitioner of medicine in this city who regularly assumed, by advertisement, the functions of a male accoucheur. He obtained confidence, notwithstanding the novelty of the attempt. Atwood knew every thing of every family; he abounded in anecdote, but his company was more courted than admired. He at one time possessed, by inheritance, great wealth, but died poor, through the conduct of his son Charles.

When Laugh and Grow Fat appeared, the public said it well fitted the case of Mortier. He was a cheerful old gentleman and paymaster to the British army; but the leanest of all human beings, according to the MS. I lately inspected of Mr. John Moore. He was almost diaphanous. Mortier built the great mansion on the Trinity Church grounds, to which I have already alluded in my account of Col. Burr's residence.

It would seem that during these times an Ode to Love was recited; the sympathetic public ascribed it to old Judge Horsmanden, so famous in the Negro Plot, who had married at seventy years of age. The Wheel of Fortune was made applicable to Governor Gage, who had arrived in this country as a captain in 1756, in the old French war, and in 1775 was commander-in-chief of the British army. The Male Coquette was by a sort of unanimous concurrence applied to James Smith, the brother of the historian of New York, the man whom I described in my sketch of Christopher Colles as writing madrigals for the young ladies. He must have pursued the game nearly half a century. When Anacreon Moore visited this city in 1802–3, Smith had the temerity to offer with renewed vigor his oblations on the altar of love. I knew him well. He was an M.D. of Leyden. When professor of chemistry in Columbia College, then called King's, his flowery diction with the students greatly disturbed both analysis and synthesis. Hempstead Plains was brought forward in those times, most probably an indigenous work. It is affirmed that it alluded to one of the prominent members of the Beekman family, Gerardus, a great sportsman, who secured the reputation of having killed more birds than any other man that ever lived. He shot deer in the city Common (now Park), and antlers, the trophies of his skill, are yet preserved among his descendants as curiosities to mark the city's progress. He kept a diary of his gunnery.

But we must hasten to times nearer our own. About the beginning of the second part of the designated one hundred years, the Morning Chronicle, a journal of much taste in literature and the arts, edited by Dr. Peter Irving, and the New York Evening Post, edited by William Coleman, were the prominent papers in which any thing like regular theatrical criticisms were published. In the former a series of articles on plays and actors was printed in 1802–3, over the signature of Jonathan Oldstyle. At the time of their appearance they were generally ascribed to the accomplished editor, Dr. Irving, who enjoyed great distinction for classical acquisition and belles-lettres knowledge. I knew him only in his advanced life, when illness had nearly exhausted his frame: yet he was most courteous, refined, and engaging. Years elapsed before the real author became known. They are, I believe, among the earliest literary efforts of our countryman, Washington Irving, then about the nineteenth year of his age. These criticisms were not wanting in free animadversion; yet betrayed something of that genial humor which so amply abounds in several of the subsequent writings of that eminent author. Coleman, a man of culture and of impulse, often supplied the city with his lucubrations, and aimed to settle all other criticisms by his individual verdict. He was often furnished with articles of peculiar merit on acting and actors, by John Wells, the renowned lawyer, by William Johnson, the well-remembered reporter, and by our lamented Anthony Bleecker. Will Wizzard, in the Salmagundi of 1807, also favored the town with two or three theatricals on the histrionic talents of the Old Park Theatre.

The arrival of Cooke in this country constitutes the great epoch in the progress of the drama, and is the period at which the historian of the American stage turns to contemplate the wonders of scenic power. On the night of the 21st of November, 1810, Cooke appeared at the Park Theatre in Richard Third, before an unprecedentedly crowded house. His vast renown had preceded him; but every anticipation was more than realized. He had reached his fifty-fourth year, yet possessed all the physical energies of thirty. The old playgoers discovered a mine of wealth in Shakspeare, now first opened. His commanding person, his expressive countenance, his elevated front, his eye, his every feature and movement, his intonations, showed the great master who eclipsed all predecessors. His capacious intellect, his boldness and originality, at once convinced his hearers of the superiority of his study and his matchless comprehension of his great author. The critics pronounced him the first of living actors. It must suffice at this time to observe, that this remarkable man and performer, during his whole career in the several cities of the Union, sustained his dramatic reputation unimpaired. The sad infirmity which too often laid hold of him, to the casual detriment of his great abilities, was dealt with by the public more in pity than in anger ; and indeed he seemed to be at times beloved the more for the dangers he had passed.

Dunlap appears throughout his whole biography to have delighted more to record his inebriation than to unfold his great professional powers. Perhaps it was easier to describe a debauch than to analzye the qualities of a sublime genius.

At this late date, after a lapse of nearly half a century, it might be pronounced foolishness to offer even a passing remark on Cooke's peculiar merits in portraying individual character. Cibber has said, the momentary beauties flowing from an harmonious elocution, cannot, like those of poetry, be their own record, and everybody has felt the force of the observation. I had seen little of the stage before I saw Cooke, and must therefore hold in comparison in the little that I utter, the impressions experienced from actors of a later date. Cooke's Shylock, a new reading to the western world, was a most impassioned exhibition. His aquiline nose was of itself a legacy here. The revengeful Jew made his great and successful impression with Tubal, and in the trial scene his triumph was complete. Iago, with Cooke, was a more palpable and consummate villain than with any other actor I have subsequently seen. I think I have seen a better Macbeth; the transitions of Cooke were scarcely immediate enough for the timid, hesitating, wavering monarch. His Sir Giles Overreach was not so terrifically impressive as that of Kean. His Kitely was an intellectual repast. His Lear verified the opinion of Johnson concerning that tragedy. "There is no play," says he, "which so much agitates our passions and interests our curiosity." Cooke's Sir Pertinax, for comic force, versatility of features, blandishments, inimitable pliability

10

of address, and perfect personation of character, is acknowledged to have surpassed Macklin's. A like tribute is due to his Sir Archy M'Sarcasm. I believe that no actor in any one part within the compass of the entire drama, ever excelled therein to an equal degree as did Mr. Cooke in the Scotch character. The impression created by its representation is too deep to be obliterated while one surviving witness remains. It was his greatest performance, and was rendered the more acceptable by his wonderful enunciation of the Scotch dialect. In one of my medical visits to him at the Old Tontine, his first residence in New York, I incidentally spoke to him concerning his personation of Sir Pertinax, and stated all the town had concluded he was a Scotchman. "They have the same opinion of me in Scotland," said he; "I am an Englishman." And how, sir, did you acquire so profound a knowledge of the Scotch accentuation? I rejoined. "I studied more than two and a half years in my own room, with repeated intercourse with Scotch society, in order to master the Scottish dialect, before I ventured to appear on the boards in Edinburgh, as Sir Pertinax, and when I did, Sawney took me for a native. It was the hardest task I ever undertook."

Cooke justly demands a greater space than this occasion warrants; but the able critical pens of the time have commemorated his achievements, and the veteran Wood, in his personal reminiscences of the stage, has dealt with him impartially and delineated his character with great fidelity. He was of a kindly disposition, of great benevolence, and filled with charitable impulses. His strong mental powers were improved by reading, yet more by observation and a study of mankind. Self-reliance was his distinguishing quality; few ever were at any time able to overcome his determination. His resolves scarcely ever yielded. When not influenced by the goblet, his conversation was instructive and his manners urbane; he had a tear for distress, and a hand of liberality for want. He was a great original, and had the logic within himself to justify innovation. His master was nature, and he would submit to no artificial rhetoric. He thought much of Kemble, and every thing of Garrick, both of whom he had seen perform. He cherished an exalted idea of his art, and demanded deference from the menial and the noble. He was thoroughly imbued with the value of Franklin's aphorism, "If you make a sheep of yourself, the wolves will devour you." He tolerated no invasion of his rights. And yet that one stain on his character, his mania for drink (a periodical disease, often of some duration), dethroned his high purpose, and at times degraded him below the dignity of man. In that condition no violence was like his; abuse of kindest friends, extravagance beyond limits, obstinacy invincible. On the return of right reason, he would cast a withering glance at those around him, and ask, "What part is George Frederick Cooke placarded for to-night?"

After one of those catastrophes to which I have alluded, I paid him a visit at early afternoon, the better to secure his attendance at the theatre. He was seated at his table, with many decanters, all exhausted, save two or three appropriated for candlesticks, the lights in full blaze. He had not rested for some thirty hours or more. With much ado, aided by Price the manager, he was persuaded to enter the carriage waiting at the door to take him to the play-house. It was a stormy night. He repaired to the green-room, and was soon ready. Price saw he was the worse from excess, but the public were not to be disappointed. "Let him," says the manager, "only get before the lights and the receipts are secure." Within the wonted time Cooke entered on his part, the Duke of Gloster. The public were unanimous in their decision, that he never performed with greater satisfaction. As he left the house, he whispered, "Have I not pleased the Yankee Doodles?" Hardly twenty-fours after this memorable night, he scattered some $400 among the needy and the solicitous, and took refreshment in a sound sleep.

Throbbing invades the heart when narrating the career of this extraordinary man, of herculean constitution, so abundant in recuperative energies; of faculties so rare, and so sublime, cut off so early. I was with him at his closing hours; serous effusion of the chest and abdomen were the immediate cause of his death. He was conscious to the last. Cooke attracted a mighty notice when with his dignified mien and stately person, attired as the old English gentleman, he walked Broadway. His funeral was an imposing spectacle. The reverend the clergy, the physicians, the members of the bar, officers of the army and navy, the literati and men of science, the members of the dramatic corps, and a large concourse of citizens moved in the procession. My worthy friend, George B. Rapelye, is the only survivor of the long train, whom I can now call to mind. The quiet Sabbath added to the solemnity. He had no kindred to follow in the procession, but there were many real mourners. The sketches of Mr. Cooke in the Dramatic Mirror of Philadelphia, executed by Leslie, then a boy, are of most remarkable fidelity.

The professional triumphs of Cooke led Holman soon after to visit America. He arrived in 1812, and saw his old friend on his dying bed. Holman had a checkered career. He was an Oxford scholar. On assuming the civilian's gown, he delivered with great success a Latin oration; the *eclat* which followed his oratorical displays at the Soho Academy, led him to abandon theology and adopt the stage. He made a great hit in Orestes, and his appearance in Romeo was a decided triumph. His Lord Townley won him most applause in New York, and was deemed a finished performance. The elegant scholarship of Holman, his rigid temperance, surpassing all I had seen in any other person, and his fidelity to all obligations, secured him a consideration which enhanced the moral estimation of the dramatic corps. Impaired health led him to seek relief at the watering-place, Rockaway, where he was seized with a fatal apoplexy, in August, 1817. The journals abroad stated that he lost his life by one of those remarkable phenomena which sometimes signalize our climate, a sort of epidemical lightning, by which himself and several of his family were stricken down. We gave him a village funeral, most respectable in numbers, at the head of which, with due solemnity, walked the long-remembered old Joseph Tyler, the comedian, who has often trod the stage with Garrick, and Charles Gilfert, the musical composer.

There are about this period of the drama, associated with Cooke, many theatrical celebrities, whose names might justly find a record here: many whom the critics lauded, and the spectators admired. Among the foremost is John Howard Payne, the American Roscius, who was signalized for his Norval, and his playing Edgar to Cooke's Lear. As an author, Payne's Brutus, and his Home Sweet Home, have secured him a world-wide renown. I became acquainted with him as the editor of the Thespian Mirror, when he was about thirteen years of age. A more engaging youth could not be imagined; he won all hearts by the beauty of his person, and his captivating address, the premature richness of his mind, and his chaste and flowing utterance. But I will abstain from further notice of him on this occasion; every reader enamored of the story of his eventful life, with the vicissitudes of authorship, of playwrights, and of actors, will satisfy his desires by turning to the instructive pages of Duyckincks' Cyclopædia of American Literature.

A list of the most popular actors, male and female, of that period, and of some subsequent years, would necessarily include Jefferson, Simpson, Wood, Hogg, Hilson, Barnes, Bernard, the Placides, Conway, James Wallack, Mrs. Oldmixon, Mrs. Johnson, Miss Johnson, Mrs. Wheatley, Mrs. Darley, Mrs. Gilfert, and Mrs. Holman. As prominent in this long catalogue, James Wallack might be permitted to stand first, as a tragedian of powers, and as a comic performer of remarkable capabilities. His Shaksperian range and his Dick Dashall are enough for present citation. Wallack is still with us, and continues as the connecting line between the old and new order of theatrical affairs. The acting drama of these times, fairly set forth, would also introduce that distinguished American, James Hackett, whose Falstaff has been the theme of applause from even the lips of fastidious critics, and whose Yankee characters have stamped his powers with the bold impress of originality. Moreover, Hackett, in his correspondence on Hamlet with that able scholar, John Quincy Adams, has given us proofs that he had trained himself in a deep study of the philosophy of Shakspeare. It would not be unprofitable to dwell upon the capabilities of Edmund Simpson, whose range of characters was most extensive, and whose talents manifested deep penetration in a broad expanse of dramatic individualities. But all this, and a thousand other circumstances, we must forego. I may be justified in remarking that, professionally, I became acquainted with a majority of these players, and can testify to the repeated evidences they afforded, from time to time, of their charitable feelings for the relief of suffering humanity, and their excellent principles in the conduct of life. At a little later date we find the boards enriched by George Bartley and his wife, formerly a Miss Smith, to whom Moore dedicated a series of his Irish melodies. His Autolychus, his Sir Anthony Absolute, and his Falstaff, will long hold possession of the memory, and Mrs. Bartley, enacting the Ode on the Passions, was a consummation of artistic skill equally rare and entrancing.

Still a little later, and a flood of histrionic talents seems almost to have overwhelmed us, in the persons of Kean, Matthews, and Macready. He who would draw the veritable portraiture and histrionic powers of these remarkable men, might justly claim psychological and descriptive instincts of the highest order. They were not all of equal or of like merits. They were all, however, elevated students, under difficulties, and long struggled against the assaults of a vituperative press and an incredulous public; they all in the end secured the glories of a great success. With Kean I may say I was most intimate. He won my feelings and admiration from the moment of my first interview with him. Association and observation convinced me that he added to a mind of various culture the resources of original intellect; that he was frank and open-hearted, often too much so, to tally with worldly wisdom. I was taught by his expositions in private, as well as by his histrionic displays, that the great secret of the actor's art depended upon a scrutinizing analysis of the mutual play of mind and matter, the reflex power of mental transactions on organic structure. His little, but well-wrought, strong frame, seemed made up of a tissue of nerves. Every sense appeared capable of immediate impression, and each impression having within itself a flexibility truly wondrous. The drudgery of his early life had given a pliability to his muscular powers that rendered him the most dexterous harlequin, the most graceful fencer, the most finished gentleman, the most insidious lover, the most terrific tragedian. The Five Courts could not boast a more skilful artist of the ring, and Garrick, if half that is said be true, might have won a grace from him. He had read history, and all concerning Shakspeare was familiar to him: times, costumes, habits, and the manners of the age. He had dipped into phrenology, and was a physiognomist of rare discernment. His analysis of characters who visited him, to do homage to his renown, often struck me with astonishment. His eye was the brightest and most penetrating any mortal could boast, an intellectual telegraph. Dr. Young, borrowing, I suppose, from Aristotle, says that terror and pity are the two pulses of tragedy; that Kean had these at command, every spectator of his Richard and Sir Giles, of his Lear and his Othello, is ready to grant. His transitions from gay to grave, yielded proofs of his capacity over the passions. He knew almost instinctively the feelings of the house, whether an appreciating audience was assembled or not, and soon decided the case, often by the earliest efforts he wrought. He was proud as the representative of Shakspeare, but told me a hundred times that he detested the profession of the actor. He loved Shakspeare, though the hardest study to grapple with, because, among other reasons, when once in memory he was a fixture, his language, he added, was so stickable. Though I was with him almost daily during his visits among us, I never knew him to look at the writings of the great poet, save once with King John, for any preparation for the stage, excepting on some two or three occasions; he never attended rehearsals, and yet, during all his performances here, he never once disappointed the public, even when I knew him suffering from bodily ills that might have kept a hero on his couch. There is something marvellous in that function, memory. Dugald Stewart was astounded when Henderson, after reading a newspaper once, repeated such a portion as seemed to him wonderful.

A like occurrence took place with our Hodgkinson. He made a trifling wager that within an hour he could commit to memory a page of a newspaper, cross reading, and he won. Kean told me that the parts of modern dramas, such, for example, as De Montfort, Bertram, and the like, could not thus be retained. Henderson told Dugald Stewart that habit produced that power of retention. Has the memory, like that peculiar faculty of calculation which Zera Colburn possessed, some anomalous function not yet unravelled?

It is well known that Kean, at one period of his histrionic career, enjoyed the unbounded admiration of the Scotch metropolis; and it is recorded that the Highland Society honored him with a magnificent sword for his highly wrought performance of Macbeth. He on several occasions adverted to the circumstance of old Sir John Sinclair's flattering correspondence on the subject. Kean, if report be true, was invited to a choice meeting at Edinburgh, where were summoned many of the philosophers, professors, and critics usually congregated in that enlightened city. Scott and Wilson, I take it, were of the number, headed by the octogenarian, Henry Mackenzie, the "Man of Feeling," president of the Highland Society. It was easy to foresee, that such an opportunity would not be permitted to escape such a scholastic board without some interrogatories being put to the great dramatic hero, on the genius of Shakspeare, and on the eloquence which elucidated him. The old professors of rhetoric had too long handled the square and compass in their Chiromania not to feel desirous of hearing if some new postulates might not be assumed, whose excellence might advance their science. My old friend, John Pillans, of the High School, broached the subject. Kean had little to disclose; yet that little had to suffice. He had no harangue on eloquence to deliver. He maintained that Shakspeare was his own interpreter, by his intensity and the wonderful genius of his language. Shakspeare, he continued, was a study; his deep and scrutinizing research into human nature, and his sublime and pathetic muse, were to be comprehended only by a capacity alive to his mighty purposes. He had no rhetorician's laws to expound. If a higher estimate was at any time placed upon his performances than upon those of some others who fulfilled the severe calling of the actor, he thought it might be due in part to the devotion which he bestowed on the authors, and the conceptions engendered by reflection. I have overlooked, said he, the schoolmen, and while I assume no lofty claims, I have thought more of intonation than of gesticulation. It is the utterance of human feelings which rises superior to the rules which the professor of rhetoric enjoins. It is the sympathy of mental impression that acts. I forgot the affections of art, and relied upon the emotions of the soul. It is human nature that gives her promptings.

I interrogated Kean, at one of those intellectual recreations which now and then occurred in New York, if no other writer could be pointed out whose language might awaken similar emotions by elucidation. The funeral service of the Church, he replied, will demonstrate the capabilities of the speaker. When a new candidate for histrionic patronage waits at Old Drury, he is perhaps tested by the committee to declaim the speech over the dead body of Cæsar, or the opening address of Richard the Third, or perhaps something from that mawkish lover, Romeo; or he may be requested to read a portion of the funeral service of the Church; this last answers as well as any thing from Shakspeare. We have nothing higher in eloquence; nothing more effective, and the qualifications of the speaker are often by such a criterion determined upon. I myself shall only add that Kean was controlled by an inherent sagacity, and, as events proved, that sagacity was convincing. The turmoils of the mind which led to such results, he could not expound. Aided by a masterly judgment, he knew where the golden treasures of the poet were buried, and his genius knew how and when to bring them to light, and to give them their peculiar force.

Kean's success was not equal in all characters, and he frankly declared it. But how often has this proved to be the case with others! Kemble could not excel in Richard the Third nor in Sir Edward Mortimer, and Kean could not approach the excellence of Kemble's Coriolanus. Miss O'Neil, when she played Mrs. Haller, proved that the pathetic had never entered the bosom of Mrs. Siddons. Kean's scope was too wide for any mortal to cherish a design so presumptuous as universal success; but the impartial and well-informed historiographer of the stage will allow, that no predecessor in Kean's vocation ever excelled in so great a degree in such numerous and diversified delineations of the products of the dramatic art. And to what cause for such success are we to look, but to that vast capacity which original genius had planted within him; to that boldness that dreaded not a new path, to that self-reliance which trained him, by untiring industry, to his assigned duty; to that confidence which he cherished, that the artificial school of form and mannerism, with its monotonous tone, was rebellious to flexible nature, and must in time yield to those diviner agents residing in the human breast? In the mechanics of ordinary life there might be such laws, and admiration excited at the regularity of the pendulum, but the intellectual was a subtle ether not to be thus controlled. The service in which he had enlisted, as interpreter and expositor of the Bard of Avon, demanded that the passions have fair play, and that it were an absurdity to restrain the emotions of the soul by the laws of the pedagogue. His head was his prompter—his mental sagacity his guide. Never has an actor appeared who owed less to the acting of others; he disdained imitation; he was himself alone. Need we have doubted the ultimate success of such heroism?

How vastly is his merit enhanced when we consider the renowned individuals who had had possession of the stage for some one or two ages prior to his entrēe in London, whose memories still lingered there, and further recollect the abilities of those, too, who, at the very time when he made his debut at Old Drury, were still the actual properties of the dramatic world, and had secured the homage of the British nation: the Kembles, Young, Mrs. Siddons, and we may add, Miss O'Neil. The verdict had gone forth that these artists could do no wrong; yet the little man, who had feasted sumptuously on herring at a shilling a week, who had studied Shakspeare at the Cock and Bottle, who had enacted him amidst the clanking chains of a prison, appears as Shylock. The actors and the audience, one and all, dismiss every doubt; a new revelation is unfolded, and the intellect of the most intellectual critics is exhausted in ink and paper in laudation; the polyglott is ransacked for new phrases of approbation. The little man, but mighty actor, assumes a succession of Shaksperian characters, and London is taken, as if by storm. Hazlett declares that Mr. Kean's appearance is the first gleam of genius breaking athwart the gloom of the stage; the dry bones shake, and the mighty Kemble exclaims, "He acts terribly in earnest!" Coleridge says, "To see Kean act is reading Shakspeare by lightning;" and Byron, the immortal bard, bursts forth:

———— "Thou art the sun's bright child!
The genius that irradiates thy mind
Caught all its purity and light from heaven.
Thine is the task, with mastery most perfect,
To bind the passions captive in thy train!
Each crystal tear, that slumbers in the depth
Of feeling's fountain, doth obey thy call!
There's not a joy or sorrow mortals prove,
Or passion to humanity allied,
But tribute of allegiance owes to thee.
The shrine thou worshippest is Nature's self—
The only altar genius deigns to seek.
Thine offering—a bold and burning mind,
Whose impulse guides thee to the realms of fame,
Where, crowned with well-earned laurels, all thine own,
I herald thee to immortality."

To demonstrate that his empire was not alone Shakspeare and the lofty tragic writers, he assumed comedy; he gave us the Duke Aranza, Octavian, Sylvester Daggerwood, Luke, etc., and played Paul, Mungo, and Tom Tug, exhibiting the variety and extent of his dramatic capabilities without loss of his mighty fame as the greatest living tragedian. I attribute Kean's unrivalled success in so wide a range of characters somewhat to his extraordinary capacity for observation. He individualized every character he assumed —we saw not Mr. Kean. Wherever he was, he was all eye, all ear. Every thing around him, or wherever he moved, fell within his cognizance.

He might have been called the peripatetic philosopher. He was curious in inquiring into causes. He echoed the warbling of birds, the sounds of beasts, imitated the manner and the voices of numerous actors; studied the seven ages, and said none but a young man could perform old King Lear; was a ventriloquist, sang Tom Moore's Melodies with incredible sweetness, and was himself the composer of several popular airs. Thus qualified, he drew his materials fresh from observations amid the busy scenes of life, where he was ever a spectator. Garrick declared that he would give a hundred pounds to utter the exclamation "Oh!" as did Whitfield. What might he not have given to pronounce the curse on Regan as did Mr. Kean, or to be able to rival the pathos of his Othello?

The Lake Poets, as they were called, took a new road in their strides towards Parnassus, but that road is now mainly forsaken, and remains almost unvisited. Kean, with loftier aspirations and still more daring, essayed a new reading of Shakspeare; there was large by-play, but no still life in him; he rejected the monotonous and soporific tone; he left the artificial cadence and the cold antique to Kemble. The passions with which the Almighty has gifted mortals were his reliance, and as these will last while life's blood courses through the heart, so long will endure the histrionic school which Kean founded.

That Kean's first visit to the United States was a complete triumph none will deny; that his second, after his disasters in London, by which his own folly and crime had made him notorious, now rendered the American people less charitable to his errors, and less cordial in their support of his theatrical glory, is also an admitted fact; yet his return among us gave demonstrations enough to prove that his professional merits were still recognized as of the highest order: he might have repined at the departure of those halcyon days of 1820–21, yet there were testimonials enough nightly accompanying his career in 1825–26, to support him in his casual sinking of the spirits, and perhaps at times to nullify that contrition that weighed so heavily at the heart. His devotion as an actor was not less earnest than when I first knew him. His Sir Giles in New York abated not of the vehemence and terror that characterized it as I had witnessed it at Old Drury in London, in 1816. There were sometimes with him moments of renewed study, and he threw himself into several new characters which he had not previously represented here; his Zanga, his De Montfort, and Paul were of the number. His Othello was received with louder plaudits than ever, and his Lear, as an inspiration beyond mortals, was crowned with universal praises. Kean often told me that he considered his third act in Othello his most satisfactory performance within the range of his histrionic career. "Such," I said, "seems to be the public verdict; yet I have been more held in wonder and admiration at your King Lear." "The real insanity and decrepitude of that old monarch, of fourscore and upwards," said Kean, "is a most severe and laborious part. I often visited St. Luke's and Bethlehem hospitals in order to comprehend the manifestations of real insanity ere I appeared in Lear. I understand you have an asylum for lunatics; I should like to pay it a visit, and learn if there be any difference in the insanity of John Bull and of you Americans." He was promised an opportunity.

A few days after, we made the desired visit at Bloomingdale. Kean, with an additional friend and myself, occupied the carriage for a sort of philosophical exploration of the city on our way thither. On the excursion he remarked he should like to see our Vauxhall. We stopped; he entered the gate, asked the doorkeeper if he might survey the place, gave a double somerset through the air, and in the twinkling of an eye stood at the remote part of the garden. The wonder of the superintendent can be better imagined than described. Arriving at the Asylum, with suitable gravity he was introduced to the officials, invited to an inspection of the afflicted inmates, and then told, if he would ascend to the roof of the building, a delightful prospect would be presented to his contemplation: many counties, and an area of sea, rivers, and lands, mountains and valleys, embracing a circuit of forty miles in circumference. His admiration was expressed in delicious accents. "I'll walk the ridge of the roof of the Asylum!" he exclaimed, "and take a leap!" and forthwith started for the gable end of the building; "it's the best end I can make of my life." Forthwith he started towards the western gable end. My associate and myself, as he hurried onward, seized him by the arms, and he submissively returned. I have ever been at a loss to account for this sudden freak in his feelings; he was buoyant at the onset of the journey; he astonished the Vauxhall doorkeeper by his harlequin trick, and took an interest in the various forms of insanity which came before him. He might have become too sublimated in his feelings, or had his senses unsettled (for he was an electrical apparatus), in contemplating the mysterious influences acting on the minds of the deranged, for there is an attractive principle as well as an adhesive principle in madness; or a crowd of thoughts might have oppressed him, arising from the disaster which had occurred to him a few days before with the Boston audience, and the irreparable loss he had sustained in the plunder of his trunks and valuable papers, while journeying hither and thither on his return to New York. We rejoiced together, however, when we found him again safely at home, at his old lodgings, at the City Hotel. I asked him in the evening how he studied the phases of disordered intellect; he replied, by the eye, as I control my lion. I cannot do better with this part of my subject than quote from an able article on Kean's Lear, as it appeared in Blackwood. Of this most genuine of his performances of Shakspeare, the writer says: "The genius of Shakspeare is the eternal rock on which the temple of this great actor's reputation must now rest; and the 'obscene birds' of criticism may try in vain to reach its summit and defile it, and the restless waves of envy and ignorance may beat against its foundation unheeded, for their noise cannot be heard so high."

There are a thousand stories afloat concerning Kean.* I shall swell the number with one or two derived from personal knowledge. The criticisms of the American papers on his acting were little heeded by him; he said after an actor has made a severe study of his character he feels himself beyond the animadversions of the press. While here, however, a periodical was published by the poet Dana, called the "Idle Man." A number, in which his dramatic talents were analyzed, was placed in Kean's hand; having read it deliberately, he exclaimed, with much gratification, "This writer understands me; he is a philosophical man; I shall take his work across the water." On several alternate nights he played the same round of characters with the distinguished Cooper; and two parties were naturally created by it. He soon saw that Cooper had his friends, and noticing the caption of the respective papers, after one or two successive days, he ordered his man Miller regularly to handle the opposition gazette with a pair of tongs, and con-

* The professional receipts of Kean during his engagement in New York, were, I believe, at least equal to those for a like number of nights which he received at the acme of his renown in London. His average income for some twelve or fifteen years was not less than ten thousand pounds per annum. He rescued Old Drury from bankruptcy, yet he is said to have been often in need, and died almost penniless. There was no one special extravagance chargeable to him; but he was reckless in money matters, and figures entered not into his calculations. He had a helping hand for all applications. As in the case of Quin, the needy found in him a friend. The noble conduct of his son Charles is familiarly known; but no language can plead in extenuation of the deplorable prodigality of the elder Kean.

vey it away from his presence. He said he never read attacks.

Kean had early determined to erect a monument to the memory of the actor he most esteemed, George Frederick Cooke. We waited upon Bishop Hobart for permission to carry out the design. Kean struck the attention of the bishop by his penetrating eyes and his refined address. "You do not, gentlemen, wish the tablet inside St. Paul's?" asked the bishop. "No, sir," I replied, "we desire to remove the remains of Mr. Cooke from the strangers' vault and erect a monument over them on some suitable spot in the burial-ground of the church. It will be a work of taste and durability." "You have my concurrence then," added he. But I hardly knew how we could find a place inside the church for Mr. Cooke." The monument was finished on the 4th of June, 1821, the day Mr. Kean terminated his first visit to America. He repaired in the afternoon to pay his last devotion to it. He was singularly pleased with the eulogistic lines on Cooke; tears fell from his eyes in abundance, and as the evening closed he walked Broadway, listened to the chimes of Trinity, returned again to the churchyard, and sang, sweeter than ever, "Those Evening Bells," and "Come o'er the Sea." I gazed upon him with more interest than had ever before been awaked by his stage representations. I fancied (and it was not altogether fancy) that I saw a child of genius on whom the world at large bestowed its loftiest praises, while he himself was deprived of that solace which the world cannot give, the sympathies of the heart.

Towards the close of his second visit to America,

Kean made a tour through the northern part of the State, and visited Canada; he fell in with the Indians, with whom he became delighted, and was chosen a chief of a tribe. Some time after, not aware of his return to the city, I received, at a late hour of the evening, a call to wait upon an Indian chief, by the name of Alantenaida, as the highly-finished card left at my house had it. Kean's ordinary card was Edmund Kean, engraved; he generally wrote underneath, "Integer vitæ scelerisque purus." I repaired to the hotel, and was conducted up stairs to the folding-doors of the hall, when the servant left me. I entered, aided by the feeble light of the room; but at the remote end I soon perceived something like a forest of evergreens, lighted up by many rays from floor-lamps, and surrounding a stage or throne; and seated in great state was the chief. I advanced, and a more terrific warrior I never surveyed. Red Jacket or Black Hawk was an unadorned, simple personage in comparison. Full dressed, with skins tagged loosely about his person, a broad collar of bear-skin over his shoulders, his leggings, with many stripes, garnished with porcupine quills; his moccasons decorated with beads; his head decked with the war-eagle's plumes, behind which flowed massive black locks of dishevelled horse-hair; golden-colored rings pendant from the nose and ears; streaks of yellow paint over the face, massive red daubings about the eyes, with various hues in streaks across the forehead, not very artistically drawn. A broad belt surrounded his waist, with tomahawk; his arms, with shining bracelets, stretched out with bow and arrow, as if ready for a mark. He descended his throne and rapidly approached me. His eye was meteoric and fearful, like the furnace of the cyclops. He vociferously exclaimed, Alantenaida! the vowels strong enough. I was relieved; he betrayed something of his raucous voice in imprecation. It was Kean. An explanation took place. He wished to know the merits of the representation. The Hurons had honored him by admission into their tribe, and he could not now determine whether to seek his final earthly abode with them for real happiness, or return to London, and add renown to his name by performing the Son of the Forest. I never heard that he ever afterwards attempted, in his own country, the character. He was wrought up to the highest pitch of enthusiasm at the Indian honor he had received, and declared that even Old Drury had never conferred so proud a distinction on him as he had received from the Hurons. My visit was of some time. After pacing the room, with Indian step, for an hour or more, and contemplating himself before a large mirror, he was prevailed upon to change his dress and retire to rest. A day or two after, he sailed for Europe, with his Indian paraphernalia.

I have said nothing of the intemperate habits, or of the extravagance and profuse liberality of Kean. That word intemperate is to be viewed in various lights, and with much qualification. The old proverb, that what is one man's food is another's poison, has much of fact in it. Viewing, moreover, intemperance as among the greatest calamities that afflict mortals, I should sadden in my soul if a word proceeded from my lips that might give it any quarters. But Mr. Kean's susceptibilities to impression were such that high excitement might follow two or three glasses of port. Mr. Grattan has well described the progress of that condition in Kean, and I have observed, at several times, that those Latin citations of his were ominous. Yet I never saw Mr. Kean indulge in any drink whatever, until the labors of the drama were over. That he often at other times erred, I am ready to admit. Knox, an English actor, who played Glenalvon, demanded two quarts of brandy to go through with that character in his stentorian way, and when I administered reproof to him, because of his inordinate indulgence, he only replied it was just the right measure. John Reeve, according to manager Simpson, partook still more bountifully to carry through his broad farce; but he was very bulky, and required almost a kilderkin to saturate him. The benevolence of Kean, and his charities, were almost proverbs. Another noble attribute characterized him: he was free of professional envy, and lauded rising merit. All he asked was to be announced to the public in large letters. He prognosticated the career of Forest, after seeing his Othello once. I could not dismiss Kean with more brevity. He was a meteor in the dramatic firmament. I might have added much more. The classical Tuckerman, in his Biographical Essays, has given us an admirable exposition of the philosophy of the man and his acting, and Proctor has done well with him, but might have done better. I shall say less of Mathews and Macready.

Hemmed in as I am by time and circumstances, I am compelled to restrict my observations on Charles Mathews, a man of extraordinary faculties, who had secured a prodigious renown in his vocation ere his arrival in the American States, and which reputation was increased by his public displays in this country. He was a remarkable specimen of what early training and study may accomplish. His very physical defects yielded to him special advantages. His close observation, his susceptible nervous system, his half hypochondriacal temperament, sharpened a natural acuteness, which, with uninterrupted devotion, led to results of the most commanding regard. If ever triumph was secured by speciality, it was eminently so in the case of Mathews. He studied occurrences with the severity of philosophical analysis. Attitudes, the lear of the eye, the motion of the lip, the crook of the fingers, the turn of the toe, the ringlet of a lock, intonation of voice, every demonstration of emotion or passion, came within the scope of his capabilities. The characteristics of divers nations marking every condition of varied life, from the dignity of the Plenipo to the servitude of the menial, were all caught by him, and you looked in turn to him for the verisimilitude of every delineation he attempted. The brooding cadence of the cooing dove, and the hideous braying of the donkey, were equally at the command of his versatile talents. He was, in short, the master of mimic power, and used it with unparalleled effect. In comedy he was the acknowledged head in numerous parts. His Goldfinch is represented to me, by experienced theatrical goers, to have surpassed that of Hodgkinson; his Lord Ogilby, his Morbleau, his Coddle, and many other portraitures, still remain in vivid recollection. His "At Home" proved him, indeed, the actor of all work, and with the American community, yielding to the persuasions of friends, he evinced the extraordinary capacity that Othello could be enacted by him with signal success.

If it be asked how came Mathews the possessor of such rare gifts, I answer they were derived from a nervous susceptibility of the most impressible order, from intense study, and the cultivation of elegant literature. He read largely; he was quickened into observation by every phase of varied life, and his morbid constitution never forsook him, or tolerated indifference to surrounding objects. Like an homeopathic patient he was never well—always complaining, and ever on the look-out, with this difference, however, that while the narcotized victim seems incessantly in search of physical improvement, Matthews seemed ever to be busy in intellectual progress. With the dexterity of an archer he aimed at characteristics wherever they might be found, and made the peculiarities of individuals the pledge of his skill. Abroad he sought out John Philpot Curran, and embodied both the manner and thoughts of the orator most faithfully. In this country he looked out for the great Irish orator, Thomas Addis Emmet, and unconsciously, to the great pleader, took him to the life, in manner and in tone, with transcendent effect. Had that jurist lived in these latter days, with spiritualism and clairvoyance running mad, he might have concluded himself to have been translated into some other individuality.

His arrival in New York occurred in September, 1822; the yellow fever was prevailing. I received a kind note from that benevolent man, Simpson, the manager of the Park Theatre, to hasten on board a ship off the harbor, in which was Mr. Mathews, in mental distress at the prospect of landing. The phenomena exhibited by his nervous temperament were most striking: he had been informed that one hundred and forty deaths had occurred on that day. Though some three miles off the battery, he felt, he affirmed, the pestilential air of the city; every cloud came to him surcharged with mortality; every wave imparted from the deep exhalations of destruction. He walked the deck, tottering, and in the extremest agitation. He refused to land at the city, and insisted upon finding shelter in some remote place. Hoboken was decided upon, and thither Mr. Simpson and myself accompanied him. Some two miles from the Jersey shore, on the road towards Hackensack, Mr. Simpson found lodgings for him in a rural retreat occupied by a gardener. Here Mathews passed the night walking to and fro in his limited apartment, ruminating on his probable departure within a few hours to the world of spirits. Hoboken, as it afforded him safety, as time proved, in his extreme distress, afterwards became his favorite spot for repose during his professional toil, and very often, after his theatrical duties were discharged, he was conveyed at midnight hour to that then beautiful locality. Not a few of the suggestions which crossed his mind in contemplating the American or Yankee character, were here elaborated for his future graphic sketches in dramatic delineation.

This great comedian was well stored with knowledge, and cherished a heartfelt love for literary characters; his visit to Edinburgh, and his acquaintance with Sir Walter Scott, Terry, and other eminent men of the stage, authors, and actors, and the social circle in domestic society, in which he held a part, led him to a high appreciation of intellectual pursuits. Our Cooper, our Irving, Halleck and Dunlap, were among his favorite friends. With Dr. Hosack and the generous Philip Hone, he enjoyed many festive hours. Mathews was the first individual, I heard, who gave a pretty decisive opinion that Scott was the author of the Waverley novels; this was five years before the disclosure of the fact, by Sir Walter himself, at the Ballantyne dinner, and while we in New York were digesting the argument of Coleman, of the Evening Post, and his correspondents, who attempted to prove that such could not be the truth, and that a Major or Col. Scott, of Canada, was the actual author. The adhesion to this belief was, I believe, never broken up in the mind of Coleman. But this pertinacity was very characteristic, for what could you do with a man who contended through life that Bonaparte was no soldier; that Priestley had done the world infinitely more harm than good; that skullcap was a certain specific for the cure of hydrophobia, and that yellow fever was as contagious as the plague of Aleppo? And he held many for a while in his belief, for Coleman was pronounced by his advocates a field marshal in literature, as well as in politics. There was much of worldly prudence in the habits and demeanor of this renowned actor, and he who would comprehend the labors, self-denials, and toils of the successful competitor for histrionic distinction, might profitably study the life of Mathews. He was the apostle of temperance and circumspection.

Macready, having secured a provincial reputation, appeared on the London boards at that particular juncture in histrionic affairs when Kemble, Mrs. Siddons, and Young had left the stage, or were about to withdraw from the sphere of their labors, and when

Miss O'Neil was on the eve of closing her brilliant and most successful career. His reception was all that could be desired, and Kean, with his wonted liberality, applauded his talents. He soon assumed the Shakspearian characters, and his Coriolanus, Richard the Third, Macbeth, and his Iago, added vastly to his renown. The world, however, cannot always be devoted to Shakspeare; novelty is sought, and Macready presented a captivating example of it in his Rob Roy. He became the original representative of several of Sheridan Knowles' heroes, and his Caius Gracchus and William Tell gave still greater scope to his commanding powers. In 1826 he visited New York, and won the homage of the severest critics, by his personation of the master characters of Shakspeare, which he had enacted in London. Upon his return to the United States in 1849, he still further swelled the tide of public approbation by his King Lear and his Richelieu. The disasters which disgraced our metropolis, by the occurrence of the Astor Opera House riot, are still fresh in memory, and need not be dwelt upon. On that memorable occasion Macready gave proofs abundant of his personal prowess and undaunted spirit. Mr. Macready has made three visits to the United States—in 1826, 1844, and 1849—and has been received at each visitation with an increased public approbation.

To analyze the wide range of the drama which the professional life of Macready embraced, would be presumptuous, and is not within our power; we are, moreover, merely touching some of the leading incidents in the histrionic movements of this city, and are exempt from the obligations which an address to the

Dramatic Association might impose. Mr. Macready is less of a comedian than tragedian, but in this latter, the materials are ample to demonstrate that, in the maturity of his faculties, his efficiency justly placed him at the head of the English stage. He cannot be entirely classed with the exclusive followers of nature, though he borrowed largely from her resources; and it would be unjust to his original powers to attribute his excellences to his adoption of the cold and formal school of actors. Hazlitt, a discriminating dramatic critic, pronounced him by far the best tragic actor that had come out, with the exception of Kean. But Mr. Macready has other and higher claims to our regard and esteem. He studied and enacted Shakspeare less for objects of pecuniary result than to bring out for increased admiration the matchless beauties and the deep philosophy of the great author in the purity of his own incomparable diction; and he made corresponding efforts to eradicate the corruptions which annotators and playwrights have introduced. He loathed the clap-traps of sentiment with which the stage was so often burthened. He was restless with the commentators. The bloated reputation of Cibber's interpolations he decried, and felt anguish at the innovations of even Dryden and Massinger. They were obstacles to the true worship of Shakspeare, and he deemed it imperative that they be overcome. We should hold no parley, he said, with critics who could pilfer an absurdity, and then profanely saddle it on Shakspeare. Assuredly he deserves all praise for his unceasing toil and his noble ambition.

Mr. Macready has been ever scrupulously careful about assuming a part in plays which tended to the exaltation of the baser passions, and the increase of licentiousness. The regularity of his own life added to the self-gratification he enjoyed from so scrupulous a line of conduct in his professional duty. Believing that a great ethical principle for the improvement of morals and the diffusion of knowledge resided in the stage, he, above all things, wished Shakspeare to be exhibited as he is, unencumbered with the trappings of other minds, and I have little doubt that in his happy retirement he finds solace in the conduct he adopted. Elegant letters occupy a portion of the leisure hours which Mr. Macready has at command since his withdrawal from theatrical toil, and the journals have recently noticed with commendation the efforts he is engaged in to enlarge the empire of thought and morals by promoting the establishment of public schools. He virtually, if recent reports be true, is at this present period a voluntary teacher of morals and science. His philanthropy has created a school for the rising generation, and even for maturer years, at his beautiful retreat, at Sherborne, in Dorsetshire. Whatever may have been the vicissitudes and trials which have oppressed at times the course of his honorable life, he will assuredly find an adequate recompense in the benevolent and grateful pursuits which now absorb so largely his experienced intellect. His late lecture on poetry, and its influence on popular education, delivered before the British Athenæum, has been read by thousands with the strongest approval.

I shall close these fragmentary observations on the drama and the players, with a quotation from a judicious criticism on the edition of Shakspeare lately published, with numerous annotations, by the Rev. H. N. Hudson. Few will dissent from the closing remarks of the able writer. Mr. Gould observes: "We cannot forbear a passing remark on the disappearance of the theatrical representatives of Shakspeare, just at the point of time when his text, in its highest attainable purity, is restored to the world. Garrick, Kemble, Siddons, Cooke, Kean, and Macready, for the greater part of a century, practically expounded the language of the poet; and the genius of the actor, co-operating with the genius of the author, unfolded to five successive generations the living realities of Shakspeare's power. These six luminaries have now all passed away; Macready alone surviving to enjoy in retirement the homage due to his public talents and private virtues. The loss of these great actors is the more to be deplored, because *their* art dies with them, and hence it is not strange that, with their professional exit, the drama itself should have declined. Shakspeare is immortal in the library; but on the stage probably few men now living will see him resuscitated."

Were my individual feelings to be consulted, I would fain dwell at some length on the introduction of the Garcia Italian opera *troupe* in this city as an historical occurrence in intellectual progress of permanent interest. It was destined to create new feelings, to awaken new sentiments in the circle of refined and social life, and its mission I believe is accomplished. The opera, whatever may be the disputes touching its origin, was known to be the offspring of genius. It had universal approval as an exalted mental recreation to recommend it; its novelty here secured prompt attention to its claims, and its *troupe* of artists who honored us with their *entrée* were considered the recognized professors of the highest order in the art. It captivated the eye, it charmed the ear, it awakened the profoundest emotions of the heart. It paralyzed all further eulogiums on the casual song-singing heretofore interspersed in the English comedy, and rendered the popular airs of the drama which had possession of the feelings, the lifeless materials of childish ignorance. Something, perhaps, was to be ascribed to fashionable emotion, for this immediate popular ascendency. For this advantageous accession to the resources of mental gratification, we were indebted to the taste and refinement of Dominick Lynch, the liberality of the manager of the Park Theatre, Stephen Price, and the distinguished reputation of the Venetian, Lorenzo Da Ponte. Lynch, a native of New York, was the acknowledged head of the fashionable and festive board, a gentleman of the ton, and a melodist of great powers and of exquisite taste; he had long striven to enhance the character of our music; he was the master of English song, but he felt from his close cultivation of music and his knowledge of the genius of his countrymen, that much was wanting, and that more could be accomplished, and he sought out, while in Europe, an Italian *troupe*, which his persuasive eloquence and the liberal spirit of Price led to embark for our shores, where they arrived in November, 1825. The old Italian poet and composer of the libretto of Don Giovanni and Le Nozze di Figaro, the associate of Mozart, was here in this city to greet them, and on the night of 29th of October, 1825, at the Park Theatre, we listened to Il Barbière de Seviglie of the matchless Rossini.

More was realized by the immense multitude who filled the house than had been anticipated, and the opera ended with an universal shout of *bravo, bravissimo.* The city reverberated the acclamations. The indomitable energy of Garcia, aided by his melodious strains and his exhaustless powers, the bewitching talents of his daughter, the Signorina Garcia, with her artistic faculties as an actress, and her flights of inspirations, the novelty of her conception, and her captivating person, proved that a galaxy of genius in a novel vocation unknown to the New World, demanded now its patronage. To these primary personages, as making up the roll, were added Angrisani, whose bass seemed as the peal of the noted organ at Haerlem; Rosich, a buffo of great resources; Crevelli, a promising *debutante;* the younger Garcia, with Signora Garcia, and Madame Barbiere with her capacious tenor, constituting a musical phalanx which neither London nor Paris could surpass, nay, at that time could not equal. From the moment that first night's entertainment closed, I looked upon the songs of Phillips (which had made Coleman, the editor, music-mad), the melodies of Moore, and even the ballads of Scotland, as shorn of their popularity, and even now I think myself not much in error in holding to the same opinion. The Italian opera is an elaboration of many thoughts, of intelligence extensive and various; while it assimilates itself by its harmonious construction and entirety, it becomes effective by external impression and rational combination. It blends instruction with delight; if it does not make heroes, it at least leads captive the noblest attributes of humanity; and had a larger forethought and wiser government watched over its destinies, it might still exist in its attractive displays as a permanent institution in this enlightened and liberal metropolis

I must add a few words on that great Maestro, Garcia. It is true that his vast reputation is secured for the future by his biographer; he was a successful teacher, a composer of many operas, and his merits as a performer are fresh in the recollections of the operatic world; but it is sometimes profitable to cast a backward glance over what we have lost. He was a native of Seville, reared in Spanish music, and in fulfilling his part in that *rôle* with enthusiam, was summoned in 1809 to Paris, where he was the first Spanish musician that appeared in that capital. Garat, on hearing him, exclaimed, "The Andalusian purity of the man makes me all alive." Prince Murat chose him as first tenor of his own chapel in 1812, at Naples. Catalini obtained him for her first tenor, 1816, in Paris. Here Rossini saw him and arranged affairs so that he appeared in the Barber of Seville, of which he was the original representative. He visited England in 1817, where his wonderful powers were still higher extolled, from his Othello and his Don Juan. In Paris our New York friend Lynch found him, and proffered inducements for him to visit America. Here his combined qualities as singer and actor, have never been equalled; his Othello, for force, just discrimination, and expression, astounding the beholder, and filling the house with raptures. His career in Mexico followed; and sad to relate, while on his return to Vera Cruz, he was beset by banditti, stripped of his clothing, and plundered of his 1000 oz. of gold (about 17,000 dollars of our money), the results of his severe earnings: penniless he finally reached Paris, to resume his professional labors. His spirits failed him not, but his musical powers were on the wane, and being the first to detect the decline of his great talents, and too honest to pass a counterfeit *note*, he left the operatic boards and died in 1836, aged fifty-eight.

From the sixth year of his age, and through life, Garcia was the arbiter of his own fortunes. He may be pronounced the restorer of Mozart and the promulgator of Rossini's matchless works. His daughter, afterwards Madame Malibran, eclipsed even the talents of her father; and her abilities are still a popular topic of conversation. She had the rare gift of possessing the contralto and the soprano. Her ardor, both as actress and as singer, exhibited almost a frantic enthusiasm. Animated by the lofty consciousness of genius, the novelty of her conceptions, her vivid pictures, her inexhaustible spirits had in no predecessor in her calling ever been equalled. She had no Farinelli for an instructor, but the tremendous energy, not to say severity of her father, brought out the faculties of her voice to the wonder of all who heard her. She may be said to have been consumed by the fire of her own genius. Her "Una Voce" and other airs reached the highest point of instrumentation, according to the opinion of the most astute judges. She has been followed by no imitator, because none could approach her. Recently with Alboni and Jenny Lind we have had a partial echo of her. Perhaps her ravishing person served to swell the tide of public approbation of her ravishing voice. She enchained eyes and ears. Her earlier (not her earliest) efforts were first appreciated at the Park Theatre, and the predictions there uttered of her ultimate victories, were fully verified on her return to England. So far American appreciation did honor to the then state of musical culture with the New Yorkers.

In my medical capacity I became well acquainted with the Garcia troupe; they possessed good constitutions and took little physic; but what I would aim at in the few remarks I have yet to make is, to show that those who are not artists little know the toil demanded for eminent success in the musical world. Some twelve or sixteen hours' daily labor may secure a medical man from want in this city of great expenses and moderate fees; more than that time may earnestly be devoted for many years to secure the fame of a great opera singer. It seemed to me that the troupe were never idle. They had not crossed the Atlantic twenty-four hours ere they were at their notes and their instruments, and when we add their public labors at the theatre, more than half of the twenty-four hours was consumed in their pursuit. A President of the United States or a Lord Chancellor methinks might be easier reared than a Malibran. I dismiss all allusion to nature's gifts and peculiar aptitudes. It is assumed that brains are demanded in all intellectual business. The simplicity of life, and the prescribed temperance of these musical people, was another lesson taught me. How many things are attended to lest the voice may suffer. A taste of claret, a glass of lemonade, eau sucrée, were all the drinks tolerated, and scarcely a particle of animal food until the opera was over, when, at midnight, a comfortable supper refreshed their exhausted spirits and gave repose to their limbs. The youth who aims at distinction in physic, in law, or in divinity, and who is at all cursed with indolence, might profit by studying the lives of these masters in song, as the naturalist philosophizes with the habits of the bee.

Many of this assembly, and particularly the ladies who now grace this audience, must well remember their old teacher, Signor Lorenzo Da Ponte, so long a professor of Italian literature in Columbia College, the stately nonogenarian whose white locks so richly ornamented his classical front and his graceful and elegant person. He falls within the compass of this imperfect address from his "lonely conspicuity," for the taste he cherished, and the industry he displayed in the cultivation of Italian letters, more than two thousand scholars having been initiated in the language of Italy by him, and he is still more interwoven with our theme by his enthusiastic efforts to establish the Italian opera with us. He was upwards of sixty years of age upon his arrival in America, but enjoyed sturdy manhood. His credentials to consideration challenged the esteem of the philosopher, the poet, and the man of letters. His long and eventful life deserves an ample record. His own Memoirs in part supply our wants, and the sketch of his life by one of the members of our Historical Society, Samuel Ward, is a grateful tribute to his character, from the pen of an accomplished scholar and competent judge of his peculiar merits. I enjoyed the acquaintance of Da Ponte some twenty years. Kelly, in his reminiscences, has given us some idea of his early personal appearance and his fanciful costume at the London opera. But his glory and inward consolation had not been attained until the Garcia troupe triumphed at New York, as erst at Vienna, in Don Giovanni. The language of Italy and her music were deeply-rooted in his heart. It was a day of lofty thought for the old patriarch, says his American biographer, when came among us Garcia with his lovely daughter, then in the morning of her renown; Rosich, the inimitable buffo; Angrisani with his tomb note, and Madame Barbiere, all led by our lamented Almaviva.* I must refer to the able articles on the introduction of the opera, written by a philosophical critic in the New York Review and Atheneum Magazine for December, 1825. They constitute a record of the social progress of this city that cannot be overlooked. Da Ponte died in New York in August, 1838, at ninety years. His remains were followed to the grave by many of our most distinguished citizens, among whom were the venerable Clement C. Moore, the Hon. G. C. Verplanck, Pietro Maroncelli, the fellow-prisoner of Sylvio Pellico, &c. That his long life created no wasting infirmity of mind was shown in a striking manner by his publication of a portion of the poet Hillhouse's Hadad, not long before his final illness, and which he beautifully rendered in Italian with scholastic fidelity. The day before his death he honored me with a series of verses in his native tongue, partly, I concluded, in token of gratitude, and partly to evince to his friends, that though speech had nigh left him his mind was still entire. He died firm in the Catholic faith, and was buried in the Roman Catholic cemetery, Second Avenue.

Vicissitudes had made Da Ponte a great observer of life; his intimate associations with Mozart, the countenance and encouragement he received from

* Dominick Lynch, Esq.

Joseph II., his acquaintance with Metastasio, the lyric poet and writer of operas and dramas in Italy, are prominent among the events of his earlier career, at which time he established his reputation as a melodramatist. It was easy to perceive, after a short interview with him, that his capacious intellect was filled with bookish wisdom. He had recitals at command for the diversity of society in which he chanced to be. He loved his beautiful Italy and was prolific in praise of her authors. He extolled Caldani and Scarpa, and had many charming stories concerning the great illustrator of sound and morbid anatomy, Morgagni. Da Ponte attended the last course of instruction imparted by that pre-eminent philosopher, who had then been professor some sixty years. On that memorable occasion, when Morgagni was to meet his class for the last time, he summoned his *cara sposa*, Signora Morgagni, a lady of noble family, and his surviving children, some ten out of fifteen whom she had blessed him with, and forming with them a group around his person, he pronounced a benediction on the University and on his class, and then appealed to his venerable wife for the fidelity of his domestic life, and to his children as the tokens of her love and affection. He was now in his ninetieth year. Da Ponte said he was never more in earnest, never more powerful, never more eloquent. Padua then lost the brightest teacher of anatomical knowledge the world possessed, and the University a name in its possession high above all others, which commanded the admiration of the cultivators of real science wherever the dignity and utility of medicine was appreciated. I am aware I have trespassed beyond my proper limits in this notice, but it was difficult to do otherwise. Perhaps at this very day, casting a look over the many schools of medicine established in this land, there is not an individual oftener mentioned in the courses of practical instruction, on certain branches, than Morgagni, though now dead more than two generations. I wished to draw a moral from the story, cheering to the devoted student in his severe toils to qualify him for medical responsibility. Morgagni, besides great professional acquisitions, was a master of elegant literature, an antiquarian of research, a proficient in historical lore. The learned associations of every order in Europe enrolled him as a member. His numerous writings, full of original discoveries, are compressed in five huge folios, and are consulted as a treasury of established facts on a thousand subjects. To his responsible duties, involving life and death, he superadded for more than sixty years his university teachings, and died at ninety with his mental faculties entire. How was the miracle wrought? In the pressure of herculanean labors, if *ennui* ever dared to approach, an Italiau lyric of Metastasio was all-sufficient for relief. By proper frugality he secured property; by a regular life he preserved health; by system and devotion he secured his immortal renown.

Thus much may suffice as an historical record of the introduction of the Italian opera in New York, and, consequently, in the United States. Let the undisputed honor belong to this city. It needs no prophetic vision to foresee that time will strengthen its power, culture render it more and more popular, and that its destiny is fixed among the noblest of the Fine Arts among us. It might add pleasure to this occasion, did time allow, to state particulars concerning the several opera companies which have favored us with their presence and their skill since the Garcia period: the Pedrotte company, that of Montressor, with Fornasari, and the memorable displays of Sontag, Caradori Allen, Grisi and Alboni: the triumphs and career of Ole Bull and of Jenny Lind would also enrich a narrative of such transactions with the liveliest incidents in proof of the liberality of the patrons of this intellectual and refining recreation in our metropolis. That cultivated gentleman and scholar, Robert Winthrop, in his Address, lately delivered at the opening of the grand musical festival at the Music Hall, has assigned to Boston the execution of the first oratorio in this country, and his researches are curious and instructive in the history of music. It would seem, from his antiquarian details, that the most memorable concert was given at King's Chapel on the 27th of October, 1789, on occasion of the visit of George Washington to Boston as the first President of the United States. Like a philosopher of true sentiment, Mr. Winthrop, among many felicitous observations, remarks, "What a continued and crowded record does the history of the world's great heart present of the noble sympathies which have been stirred, of the heroic impulses which have been awakened, of the devotional fires which have been kindled, of the love of God and love to man, and love of country, to which animation and utterance have been given by the magic power of music." This seems to me the true feeling of a man properly indoctrinated. I have heard language of like import proceed from the lips of John Quincy Adams; and Carlyle has said that music is the speech of angels, and that nothing among the utterances allowed to man is felt to be so divine.

I pass on to say a few words in relation to the progress among us of another branch of what is strictly denominated the Fine Arts and the Arts of Design. Admonished by the critical observations of Sir Arthur Martin Shee, that there is, perhaps, no topic so unmanageable as that of the arts in the hands of those who bring to its discussion only the superficial acquirements of amateur taste, I shall exercise a wise prudence in my limited notice of the subject. Antiquarian research will in vain find any proofs of the Fine Arts existing in this city ere the lapse of more than a century from its first settlement, and then the evidences of any thing like an approach towards their encouragement are hardly worth the notice. Our sedate and conservative Dutch ancestors were content with the architectural displays of the old-fashioned gable brick residence, the glazed tile roof, and the artificial china square plate, enriched with grotesque illustrations of dykes and windmills, and the prodigal son, as ornaments for the ample mantel and fire-jams. I have not forgotten the ten commandments thus illustrated as decorations of the fireplace in the humble suburban dwelling near the head of Pearl street, where I passed my earlier days, at that period of childhood when I studied with overflowing tears the mournful story of Cock Robin. Of the architecture of their churches or houses of worship, I have nothing now to say—the trespass would be too great.

About a century ago might be found, scattered here and there, as household decorations, portraits by Smybert, Copley, Pine, and old Charles W. Peale, of blessed memory, and still later, several by West, and many by Stuart. Our Jarvis, Inman, and Dunlap, are of quite a recent date. I have seen the portraits of the Hunters of Rhode Island, by Smybert; and the Washington by Pine, in the possession of the late Henry Brevoort. Smybert, considering the state of the arts at that time, possessed more than ordinary merit; and Pine, of whom I have often heard Pintard speak, has secured a peculiar reputation for fidelity in portraiture and excellence in coloring. In speaking of Smybert, our associate member, the venerable Verplanck remarks, that "he was not an artist of the first rank, for the arts were then at a very low ebb in England, but the best portraits which we have of the eminent magistrates and divines of New England and New York, who lived between 1725 and 1751, are from his pencil. Trumbull calls Smybert the patriarch of painting in America." Smybert was by birth a Scotchman. "He was the first educated artist who visited our shores," says Mr. Tuckerman. To his pencil New England is indebted for portraits of many of her early statesmen and clergy. Among others, he painted for a Scotch gentleman the only authentic likeness of Jonathan Edwards.* It was the extreme value at which Pintard estimated the productions of Pine, that led him to search so earnestly for the lost portraits of the Colden family by that artist, which you have in your gallery, and we have lately seen the value of his Garrick, from a perusal of Verplanck's interesting letter on the subject, published in the "Crayon," a periodical under the editorship of the great artist, Durand. The well-preserved portrait of Dr. Ogilvie, of Trinity Church, and now in their col-

* Biographical Essays, article Berkeley.

lection, is, I believe, by Pine. We have, therefore, evidences of his great merits to be seen in many places. Pintard represented to me that Pine was a little fellow, active, assiduous, and ambitious to excel. He had received great countenance from the family of the Hopkinsons, of Philadelphia.

We find no statuary at this early date as ornamental to our city, if we except that of the elder Pitt, which stood at the junction of Wall and William streets, and the leaden figure of George III., in the Bowling Green, both destroyed by popular violence in the incipient troubles of the Revolution.

An approach to a loftier encouragement of the Fine Arts was manifested by our civil authorities in the selection of the great American historical artist, the late Col. Trumbull, who was employed to execute, in 1790, the two life-sized paintings of Washington and of George Clinton, the revolutionary general. If we except the Sortie of Gibraltar, by the same artist, they may be pronounced emphatically the great works of this distinguished painter. I have often heard the richest praises bestowed on these artistic productions, for their remarkable fidelity to the originals, by our old patriots, who frequently honored them with a visit, and who personally were well acquainted with the subjects. I can easily imagine the feelings which glowed in the breast of this long-tried patriot and associate of the men of the revolutionary crisis when occupied with these celebrated paintings, and how the workings of the soul prompted every effort to secure satisfaction in the result. Our faithful Lossing's remarks on this work of Trumbull correspond with what I have again and again heard uttered by the men of '76. During his whole life Trumbull seems to have been controlled by the highest motives of patriotism in order to perpetuate the historical occurrences of his native country; to secure for posterity faithful and characteristic likenesses of our American heroes and statesmen, seems to have been the ultimate desire of his heart regardless of labor or expense. Great, indeed, would have been our misfortune deprived of his pictorial delineations of revolutionary times, and the graphic exhibitions of his prolific pencil of the men of the Eight Years' War.

This accomplished scholar, enlightened and unswerving patriot, eminent artist and delineator of American history, closed his honorable career in New York, in 1843, in the eighty-eighth year of his age. He was conspicuous among the old school gentlemen then among us. A few days before his death he accepted the presidency of the Washington Monument Association, recently organized in this city. He readily gave his countenance to the work. I attended him in his last illness, in consultation with his excellent physician, the late Dr. Washington, and it is curious to remark that the last word he distinctly uttered, on his dying bed, was Washington, referring to the father of his country, a name often on his lips.

It hardly falls within my design to enlarge in this place on the character and services of Col. Trumbull. The Reminiscences which he published give us the events most prominent in his career. A genuine love of country, a noble devotion to her interests in times of deep adversity, a patriotic ardor which led him, in season and out of season, amidst almost insuperable difficulties and perils to rescue the fleeting and precious materials which might give additional interest to her annals, entitle him to the admiration of all future time. We already see that the lapse of each successive day gives increased value to his labors for the student of American history. The arrival from Europe of that consummate genius, Gilbert Stuart, and his settlement in New York, in 1793, constitute another era in the progress of the Fine Arts among us. This remarkable man soon found his talents appreciated and called in requisition, and crowds of sitters delighted with his artistic abilities. Many of his portraits of that period are still to be found in the residences of our older families in this city. Stuart remained but a short while with us, yet that brief time was propitious to the arts. He had left the old world prompted by a noble impulse, and his desire to paint Washington was so great as to cause him to leave for Philadelphia to gratify his feelings, and it is, perhaps, not saying too much, that vast as is the inherent glory which encircles the name of the spotless patriot, the merits of that standard and unrivalled portrait by Stuart, have augmented even the renown of the father of his country.

The arts of design were promoted by the assiduous labors of Rembrandt Peale, a devoted scholar and an artist of wide renown, whose Court of Death is among the trophies of the pencil; and by Sharpless, of New York, whom I became well acquainted with in his after life. His likenesses, in crayon, won general commendation, and justice to his memory demands that he be placed in the foremost ranks of successful portrait-painters. The same remarks will honestly apply to Alexander Robertson.

In sculpture, at and about this time, Houdon and

Carrachi gave proofs of their mastery in their professional line.

Such was the platform on which the Fine Arts rested, when a number of the friends of liberal culture and elegant pursuits contemplated the organization of the first association in this city, under the name of the New York Academy of Fine Arts, in 1801. In 1808 it received the act of incorporation under the name of the American Academy of Fine Arts, and Chancellor Livington was chosen President, Col. John Trumbull, Vice-President; Dewitt Clinton, David Hosack, John R. Murray, William Cutting, and Charles Wilkes, directors. If we add the names of C. D. Colden, Edward Livingston, and Robert Fulton, we include in this enumeration the leading New Yorkers who, for years, were liberal in their patronage to promote the undertaking. Through the instrumentality of the American minister at the court of France, Napoleon made a valuable gift to the institution of many busts, antique statues, and rare prints. I can dwell but a moment longer on the fortunes of this Academy. After several years of trial and neglect it was revived in 1816. Certain paintings of West, which for a time were added to its collections through the kindness of Robert Fulton, sustained it for a few years longer from dissolution, while the several addresses of Clinton, Hosack, and Trumbull gave it for a season additional popularity. With the downfall of the American Academy, the National Academy of Design took its rise about 1828. S. F. B. Morse, he who has recently become so famous by his invention of the electric telegraph, was elected President, and the constitutional provisions of this association being far more acceptable to the feelings and views of a large majority of the artists than the old Academy favored, it has proved an eminently successful corporation and has aided in numerous ways the promotion of its specified objects, the Arts of Design. The devotion given to this institution by Thomas S. Cummings, in the instruction he for a series of years has imparted to students of art in the life and antique school, has also proved a constant source of gratification and improvement to the pupil in this elegant pursuit.

He who is solicitous to study historically the subject of the Fine Arts in this city, and to know their progress in other cities of the Union, will consult the work of William Dunlap, a writer of patient research, and abating the influence of occasional prejudice, a reliable authority. And could I, like Sir Walter Raleigh, compress the history of the world in a volume, I should record many things more amply, and be willing to take some notice of the Apollo Association, which, shortly after its formation, merged into the American Art Union, and which for a series of years exerted a wholesome influence in the diffusion of an improved taste, which was no less conducive to the fiscal advantage of those ingenious men most interested in the popularity of their important calling. If it be asked have the Fine Arts, during the incorporation of our Historical Society, advanced in this city under the countenance of these several institutions, it may be safely responded to in the affirmative. Great and distinctive as may have been the individual merits of many adepts, such as Allston, Vanderlyn, Peale, Durand, Cole, Waldo, Jarvis, Inman, Mount, Stearns, and others; by association a still greater power was wielded and successfully carried into operation in behalf of this branch of refined knowledge.

It is not to be concealed that some of our artists pursue their calling chiefly to secure a livelihood, yet there are many others who cherish a higher ideal; imbued with the greatest earnestness, patience, and faith, they have striven to comprehend the secrets of nature and achieve more than a temporary fame, the consciousness of original research and inspiration. In the enumeration of this class of painters, I would place A. H. Wenzler, so familiarly known by his unrivalled miniatures. For years his studies have been directed to the philosophy of colors. I borrow in part the language of a classical writer on art, who appears to comprehend the subject. "Mr. Wenzler has been convinced," (says this acute writer,) "that the illusion of distance, so requisite to landscape-painting, is not to be realized by perspective lines, but by the gradation of tints so obvious to nature. In order to demonstrate this, he has merely depicted in rough the material objects of a landscape—trees, rocks, a stream, a church, and a meadow, and over the whole, including a range of hills in the background, thrown these naturally graduated tints, from the prismatic rays in the immediate vicinity of the sun, to the cool light of the distant earth: the effect is exactly like nature; you imagine yourself gazing through an open window upon an actual scene; the distances throughout the picture are so natural that we feel, for the first time in art, an harmonious and complete aerial perspective. It opens a new sphere of artistic truth, and vindicates a hitherto un acknowledged law; it embodies in theory what Turner aimed at." An accomplished writer on the state of art in the United States, Dr. Bethune, in Putnam's Home Book of the Picturesque, in adverting to the hindrances which have operated on the progress of the Fine Arts in the early condition of America, has beautifully and truthfully expressed himself in these words: "Under the pressure of cares and struggles and urgent anxieties, there would be neither time nor desire for the cultivation of these elegant pursuits, which are the luxury of leisure, the decoration of wealth, and the charms of refinement. The Puritans and the Presbyterians together, the most influential, were not favorable to the fine arts, and the Quakers abjured them. Men living in log cabins and busied all day in fields, workshop, or warehouse, and liable to attacks by savage enemies at any moment, were indisposed to seek after or encourage what was not immediately useful. Their hard-earned and precarious gains would not justify the indulgence. There were few, or rather no specimens of artistic skill among them to awaken taste or imitation. It is, therefore, little to be wondered at if they did not show an appreciation of art proportionate to their advance in other moral respects, or that they waited until they had secured a substantial prosperity before they ventured to gratify themselves with the beautiful. The brilliant examples of West and Copley, with some others of inferior note, showed the presence of genius, but those artists found abroad the encouragement and instruction not attainable at home, thus depriving their country of all share in their fame, except the credit of having given them birth."

I incline strongly to the opinion that our country is destined to great distinction in the arts of design, as she is already acknowledged to excel in many of the most prominent and important of the mechanical arts. There is a genius throughout the land developing itself in these elevated pursuits. In steam navigation what has she not accomplished since the mighty innovation of Fulton ? in naval architecture where has she a rival ? Where shall I find room for an enumeration of her thousand discoveries and improvements (not notions) in mechanics, in the arts of husbandry, in that art of arts, printing, and in the lightning press of Hoe ? In sculpture she presents a Greenough, a Powers, a Frazee, a Clavenger, a Brown, and her wondrous Crawford, a native of this city. In painting, how rarely have happier displays of genius been furnished in modern time, than are given us by Durand, Weir, Elliot, Huntington, Bogle, Hicks, and Church. Had we room we might feel ourselves ennobled in contemplating the individual triumphs and merits of the devoted disciples of the fine arts our country has produced; but this undertaking is not at present at all imperative. The classical volume of Mr. Tuckerman, entitled "Artist Life," will prove an advantageous work to all who study the achievements of American genius and philosophize on its peculiar powers.

A striking characteristic of New York which reflects signal honor on the benevolence and humanity of her people, was early visible in her civic progress. The wholesome axioms of her primitive Dutch settlers and her cultivated Huguenots, soon led to the formation of schools for the cultivation of knowledge and the advancement of sound morals; and shortly after the commencement of her career, indeed as far back as the year 1699, when her population scarcely exceeded six thousand, Dr. McCready in his late historical address assures us, on the authority of our city's Chronicler, David Valentine, that the poor received partial relief in their own houses or in lodgings specially provided. Some twenty years after, an almshouse was erected near the spot where the City Hall now stands. This institution held its locality for some seventy years or more; with the collateral aid of a dispensary, which owed its origin chiefly to Dr. John Bard, the indigent found succor and relief. The almshouse yielded medical instruction by the clinical talents of Dr. William Moore, Dr. Richard S. Kissam, and Dr. Nicholas Romayne. In 1769 a pest-house was established for the reception of diseased emigrants, and the organization of a medical society in 1788, placed John Bard at its head as president. Through the efficient instrumentality of Drs. Peter Middleton, John Jones, and Samuel Bard, we find the New York Hospital took its rise and was chartered in 1771. In 1790 we find the first of our city dispensaries in operation; five years after commenced the rebuilding of the great city almshouse on the site of the old edifice in the Park, and which in 1812 was converted to other purposes, literary and historical, and destroyed by fire some two or three years ago. From historical data, I am authorized to state, that these several institutions yielded curative and saving benefits to multitudes of the indigent and the afflicted, under the direction of a wise supervision and the talents of able clinical direction, medical and surgical. The original faculty of physic organized by King's (subsequently Columbia) College, were among the prominent teachers and prescribers, and Bard, Clossy, Bayley, Hosack, Mitchill, Post, Crosby, and Nicholls, are to be enumerated in the number.

In 1811 was projected the ample Bellevue Hospital and Almshouse, which was rendered fit for the reception of its inmates in 1816, Dr. McCready tells us, from official records, at a cost of nearly half a million of dollars. The medical government of this great establishment was placed under a visiting or consulting physician, while the immediate attendance was confided to one or two physicians who resided in the institution. A malignant typhus or hospital fever breaking out, which made great havoc both with the patients and the doctors themselves, led to the appointment of a special committee of inquiry into errors and abuses, when Dr. Joseph M. Smith and Dr. Isaac Wood assumed the medical management. The occasion gave origin to the Fever Hospital at the recommendation of Dr. David Hosack, to which charity the febrile cases were transferred, when within a month the pestilence was happily at an end. Dr. Isaac Wood now received the appointment of resident physician of the Bellevue Hospital, and held the office seven years, with signal benefit to the public interests and to humanity, when his resignation led to the acceptance of the trust by Dr. B. Ogden. The tortuous policy of politics, however, now led to party appointments, and the evils incident to such policy flowed in with increased force; inexperience betrayed her incompetency, and the soundest whiggism and most radical democracy often proved equally ignorant of the principles of hygiene and curative measures. Typhus again resumed her work, and change became imperative. In the midst of revolutionary struggles, in order to rectify this deplorable condition the government of this great institution was at length placed under the medical discipline of

Dr. David M. Reese, as physician in chief. Justice demands that it be recorded, that this appointment led to a great reformation. Dr. Reese, during his term of office, stood forward the champion of innovation and improvement, and displayed in a noble cause a perseverance and ability which have proved of lasting benefit.

In 1849 the office of Resident Physician was abolished by the Board of Governors of the Almshouse, to whom the control of the establishment had passed, and the administration of the medical department of the Bellevue given over entirely to a Medical Board. Enlargements of this vast charity have from time to time been made commensurate to the wants of an increasing population, and advantageous improvements have been adopted, characteristic of the enlarged policy of our municipal authorities; and, were I to dwell longer on the subject, I might adopt with benefit the eulogistic language which Dr. McCready employs when speaking of the present renovated state of the edifice, its ample dimensions, the convenient disposition of its large and airy wards, supplied with every essential want for the afflicted, and its peculiarly sanative location on the borders of the East River.

The Bellevue Hospital may well be pronounced a noble rival to the finest and best conducted charities in the world. As a school of practical medicine and surgery, its claims will be conceded by all; and from my official connection with its affairs, for some years, I can testify to the disinterested zeal and benevolence and devotion which dignify its medical and surgical Board, and clinical instructors. It is due to individual zeal and professional ardor to add that the great field of medical and surgical practice which the Bellevue Hospital presents, has recently led to the formation of a museum of pathological anatomy, by Dr. J. R. Wood, one of the clinical instructors.

But where am I to stop when I have entered upon a consideration of the humane and benevolent institutions of this metropolis? the briefest notice of those alone which have been created, since the incorporation of the Historical Society, by legislative authority and individual liberality, would fill a volume. Some other occasions may be appropriated to so instructive an undertaking. Among her thousand claims to commendation, I consider the charities of this metropolitan city the noblest trophy she bears; and as I am much in the habit of connecting with her various institutions the names and promoters of those beneficent foundations, I cannot separate the blessings which have been imparted to suffering mortals during the long career of the New York Hospital, the wisdom imparted by clinical instruction to the hosts of students who have resorted thither for some two or three generations, and the triumphs of skill which the professional literature of the country records, achieved by Bayley, Post, Hosack, Kissam, Seaman, Stringham, and Mott. Memoirs of these eminent professors of the art of healing have long been before the public. Yet I could have wished that some surgical friend had delineated, with more satisfaction than has yet been done, the great career, as an operative surgeon, of Richard S. Kissam. For thirty years he was one of the surgical faculty of the New York Hospital, a station he was solicited to accept, and displayed in his art resources of practical tact and original genius.

He was emulous of surgical glory, and he obtained it. Our city had the honor of his birth; he was one of the sons of the renowned lawyer, Benjamin Kissam, who had been the legal instructor of John Jay. Young Kissam received a classical education uuder Cutting, of Long Island, and was graduated M. D. at Edinburgh in 1787. Upon receiving the doctorate he travelled over the continent, and made a visit to Zimmerman, who presented him with a copy of his work on Solitude. Horace and Zimmerman were the two authors Kissam most delighted in. His long and triumphant career leaves no possibility of doubt as to the solidity of his pretensions. Society had little attractions for him; he was absorbed in his profession. During more than twenty years he was the most popular operator the city could boast, and he was often called the man of the people. His professional liberality to the afflicted poor was a striking characteristic of his whole life; while from the affluent he demanded a becoming return for his skill. He died in November, 1822, aged fifty-nine years.

There are due, by the inhabitants of this metropolis, many obligations to the administration of the New York Hospital, for their early and incessant efforts to mitigate the horrors, and alleviate the sufferings of the insane. The loudest calls of humanity are often awakened in cases of afflicted intellect, and the solicitude which has from time to time invoked new desires for their relief, has by this institution been crowned with results cheering to the philanthropist. In 1808 the governors of the hospital erected an edifice for the exclusive use of the insane, on grounds adjacent to the south wing of their city hospital, and

Dr. Archibald Bruce was elected as physician. In 1820 the large and commodious institution at Bloomingdale, under their government, was opened for that special class of patients.* This beautiful site, with its ample buildings, is eminently fitted for the benevolent design originally projected, and De Witt Clinton secured its perpetuity by legislative grants. Among the medical prescribers to this magnificent institution have been Hosack, Neilson, Bayley, Ogden, MacDonald, and Pliny Earle. To this last-named physician, the public are obligated for valuable statistics and reports on mental alienation. When justice is done in an historical account of the Bloomingdale Asylum, the services of that prominent citizen, in acts of benevolence, the late Thomas Eddy, will be more entirely appreciated. He seized the first opportunity to enter into a correspondence with Samuel Tuke, of York, in England, learning of the success which, under moral management, had followed the treatment of the insane; and in Knapp's Life of Eddy are to be found many incidents connected with the literary and professional intercourse of these two worthy disciples of Primitive Barclay. When abroad in Europe I found that the condition of lunatic asylums, and the treatment of those suffering the tortures of a diseased mind, were subjects attracting great notice. The Report of the Inquiry instituted by Parliament was then just published, and vast abuses exposed, and I was prompted by more than a vacant curiosity to add personal facts to my reading, by the inspection of many institutions devoted to insanity, and the treatment adopted by them. I

* Hosack's Life of Clinton.

found more barbarity and indifference in the medical discipline of these lamentable subjects of insanity in the establishments in Holland, than elsewhere. At the Bicētre, in Paris, I was delighted with the fatherly care and medical tact of Pinel, now the acknowledged discoverer of the great benefits of moral management, but who, a short time before, was annoyed by the vituperations of the British press. At the retreat of Samuel Tuke, the benevolent and philosophic Quaker, I found all verified that his novel and impressive work related, and I was emboldened to write to Eddy, on the success of this important innovation on old prejudices which this institution presented. The result was that, fortified by the most gratifying testimony, the writings of Tuke and the publications of the day, with verbal details by intelligent travellers whom Eddy consulted, the moral management found the strongest advocates among the members of the Hospital Board, and demonstrative proof has multiplied itself again and again, that while the doctors' art is often indispensable to restore to right reason, yet that, in an imposing variety of cases, disturbed intellects are rendered again healthy, not so much by the prescription of drugs, as by humane treatment, and that system of management which the Retreat so advantageously enforced. Thomas Eddy will ever be remembered as the active agent in this great measure in the New World. Pathology has not as yet yielded us any great light on the grave causes of mental aberration, and the knife of the dissector has often failed to trace altered structure in the most perverted cases of lunacy. Hence we estimate at a still higher price the value of discipline, the exercise of the kindlier affections, and moral culture. When the adoption of these curative measures shall have become more general, we shall no longer hear of the flagellation of an infirm monarch, or of ponderous manacles and eternal night as articles of the materia medica. Our countryman Rush has enlarged our storehouse of facts on the diseases of the mind; and the treatise of Dr. Ray, of Rhode Island, has strengthened our philosophy on the analysis of intricate cases in juridical science.

With the bare mention of that newly-created charity, St. Luke's Hospital, now about to open its portals for the accommodation of the afflicted—an institution the offspring of Christian benevolence, aided by the outpouring liberality of our opulent citizens—with the further prospects we have before us of a Woman's Hospital, for the special relief of infirmities over which recent science has triumphed in the hands of Dr. Sims, and the cherished hopes derived from the success of our enlightened countryman, Dr. Howe, of Boston, that in due season even the forlorn idiot may be rescued, I reluctantly dismiss all further notice of the many corporations of like benevolence which flourish in this metropolis. But it is the less necessary on this occasion to notice the progress of humanity in this rapidly increasing city since the commencement of the Historical Society's labors; a partial estimate may be formed of the work that is actually done, and is doing among us, from the statement lately furnished by that accurate observer, Dr. Griscom.*

* According to a tableau which I have compiled, says Dr. Griscom, chiefly from their own published statements, there are in this city devoted to the care of the sick poor, four general hospitals, five dispensaries, two eye and ear infirmaries, one lying-in asylum, three special hospitals (on

With facts of this import before us, who will gainsay the claims of the divine art of healing to that public recognition which is yielded to the highest and most solemn of the professional labors of life? who that properly contemplates the duties, the objects, and the desires of the real physician, can prove reluctant in awarding to his responsible calling merits not surpassed by those of any other human avocation? Let the moralist and the philosopher give attention to the progress medical science has made during a period not longer than that of an ordinary human life; investigate the achievements which have marked the past

Blackwell's and Randall's Islands), several orphan asylums and prison-hospitals, besides other unenumerated charitable and penal establishments, where medical and surgical aid is rendered. In the institutions thus enumerated, there were treated in 1853, 151,449 cases of disease, of every variety. Devoted actively to the service of these patients, we find recorded the names of 169 medical men. Estimating the professional service rendered these patients at what is denominated, in the last report of one of these institutions in true mercantile phrase, the "lowest market value" (which of necessity varies in the several institutions, in consequence of the varied character of the cases) we have an aggregate of $745,458. An analysis of the circumstances connected with these services, shows that of these 169 medical men, 36 are merely boarded and lodged at the expense of the institutions, or receive pay equivalent thereto, amounting in all to $6,552; 30 of them receive salaries varying from $200 to $1,500, in the aggregate, $20,560; while the remaining 103, receive no compensation whatever. In addition to this, if we estimate the amount of *private* gratuitous advice which every medical man renders, in the emergencies of the sick poor, at the moderate rate ot $100 per annum, the number of practitioners in this city being about 900, we have a total sum of $90,000 to add to that before given, making a total of services rendered by the medical profession, in the year 1853, to the sick poor, in the City of New York, of $835,458, of which there is returned $27,112. In whatever light it may be viewed, the rendition of these services is simply the contribution of the medical profession to the support of public charity, to the full amount mentioned; it is so much saved to the taxpayers.—*Anniversary Discourse before the New York Academy of Medicine, Nov. 22d*, 1854, *by* John H. Griscom, M. D.

thirty years; learn in how many ways pestilence has been disarmed of half of her weapons; individual disorders lessened in malignity or exterminated; hygiene fortified with new capabilities; the principles of sanitary laws comprehended and applied; individual life made happier and prolonged; the health of mighty populations improved, and the great numerical increase in longevity. London is at the present day to be enumerated as first of the healthiest cities in the world; and the statistics which have been given to the public by our countryman, Dr. Campbell F. Stewart,* show us the grounds upon which life annuities may be granted to the greater advantage of the insurer, a ratio of improvement which Price, Morgan, and Finlaison, never anticipated.

Nearly all this has been accomplished by the mental activity, the science, and the philanthropy of the medical faculty. Had now this opulent city a proper sanitary commission duly organized, with our almost unequalled topographical advantages, we might boast of a population whose mortality might safely be estimated at twenty-five or thirty per cent. less than is recorded of its present inhabitants. Sad, sad indeed, is the reflection, that responsible trusts are not always confided to competent officials. The trammels of party too often defeat the best designs, and incompetency usurps the seat of knowledge. How long we are to be doomed to witness this monstrous incongruity and suffer its penalties, time alone must show.

In taking a retrospective view of the progress of medical science during the past fifty or sixty years in

* Discourse before the New York Academy of Medicine.

New York, the instructors and practitioners of the healing art have had many reasons for rejoicing. Our medical colleges have enhanced in power, and the means of enlightenment.* The collateral branches of science are unfolded by more ample apparatus, and by experiments such as in former days were wholly beyond our reach. Our medical annals are enriched with recorded evidences of great chirurgical skill, of novel and successful proofs, of wise discrimination, and of genius happily demonstrated; in the practical displays of clinical sciences, the writings of our authors have furnished lessons of instruction to the masters of the art abroad. Our medical and scientific literature is sought after with becoming deference by remote professors in foreign schools, and has the honor of translation for continental Europe. All this for a long season has been gratifying to individual pride and flattering to our character as a rising people. Yet it is not to be concealed that imposture still holds its influence among us, and that as a learned body, the medical profession is still disfigured by pretenders to its secrets; that jarring elements still disturb its harmony, and that the public, scarcely to be presumed to be the best judges of the recondite qualifications of the disciples of healing, are still molested by the artifices of the designing and the effrontery of the ignorant.

More than forty years ago I gave utterance to my opinion on the condition of the medical art in New

* Now three in number:—The College of Physicians and Surgeons, founded in 1807, its present head, Dr. Cock; the University of the City of New York, founded in 1840, present head, Dr. Draper; and the New York Medical College, founded in 1848, present head, Dr. Greene.

York.* The reasons for denunciation of many occurrences then prevalent, were stronger than at the present day. The condition of affairs is ameliorated. Numerous agencies have been in operation since that period, which have corrected many abuses detrimental to public safety. Then we could not speak of a school of Pharmacy. The Indian doctors and the effete remnant of licentiates by a justice's court, thanks to a superintending providence, now rest from their labors. Collegiate knowledge is more widely diffused, and he is an adventurous individual who now presumes to approach the bed-side without the clinical knowledge of hospitals. It may be written as an axiom, You might as well create a practical navigator by residence in a sylvan retreat, as furnish a physician without hospital experience.

* "That almost every district of our country abounds with individuals who set up to exercise the duties of practitioners of medicine need scarcely be stated; how great is the number of them, who from want of proper education and from habits of indolence, are totally ignorant of the first principles of their profession, and who degrade the noblest of studies into the meanest of arts, cannot have escaped the attention of any who at all regard the interests of society. That characters of this description do abound, not in this or that particular city or district, but are to be met with in almost every part of the country, is a fact which no one, we presume, will have the hardihood to deny. Though they differ from beasts of prey, inasmuch as these are most generally found in the uninhabited wilds of the country, while those are most abundantly congregated in our largest and most populous cities, yet they wage war with equal success as it regards the destruction of their objects. So frequently, indeed, do they present themselves to our view as almost to have become domesticated and familiar with us, and to have lost that novelty which monsters in general possess. The inroads and depredations which they commit, bid defiance to all calculation; whether they come in the natural shape of nostrum-mongers and vendors of infallible cures, or whether they assume a peculiar grimace and affected sapience, that touch us equally pestilential."
—*American Med. and Philosoph. Register*, vol. iii.

Nevertheless, it would be criminal to ignore the fact that the noble art still struggles with many difficulties, and it is a glaring truth that not the least of them has arisen in the vicissitudes of legislation. The few wholesome laws, which a century had brought forth, for the advancement of medicine and the protection of its rights, were by state authority, some ten or twelve years since, abrogated, and strange to add, the bill which accomplished that nefarious measure was introduced into the chamber of the Senate by a partisan representative from this city. The distinguished president of our Historical Society, Lieut. Gov. Bradish, was then a member of the Senate. It is scarcely necessary to add that his cultivated mind recoiled at the measure, and that his strenuous efforts were exerted to defeat the iniquitous law. There was no monopoly existing to absorb the rights of others that could justify such enactment. The colleges did no more than confer their usual honors, to distinguish and reward merit; they fostered rising talent, and held communion with mature experience, with no other aim than to exalt excellence; their very incorporation forbade their countenance of corrupt practices, and with the principles ever inherent in disciplined minds, they disdained to mar the rank of professional worth. I have often had my credulity taxed to believe that in these enlightened days such hardihood could have been exhibited by the makers of our laws, and that too at the very seat of wisdom, where our special guardians of literature and science, the Hon. the Regents of the University, annually convene, and where, moreover, that long created association, the State Medical Society, with its many able members, are wont to exercise their chartered privileges for medical improvement.

It is almost superfluous to remark that the memorable act to which I have alluded was received by the profession with emotions of sorrow and indignation. It was now seen that the noble art was again left unprotected by the representatives of the people, and consequently by the people themselves. It had thus found itself in the beginning of the city, but a revolving century had presented some relief; its prospects had brightened, and the rights and immunities of the regular physician had been recognized, and approved laws had secured him against the tricks of the harlequin and the wiles of the over-reaching. The disciplined medical man is not, however, the easiest to be disheartened. His study is human nature, and he comprehends its phases.

Intus et in cute novi.

He is familiar with hindrances, and in the exercise of his art has often prescribed for individual mental delusion, and can comprehend the sources of popular error. What is sporadic he knows may become epidemic.

The medical faculty, accordingly, now took a new view of the interests of their profession and the safety of the people. Their determination was fixed that no degeneracy in that science to which their lives were devoted, should follow as a consequence of pernicious legislation. Notwithstanding all restrictions of qualifications for the exercise of the art might be considered as removed, yet the city was not to be dismayed by absurd enactments, nor the profession alarmed because the door was opened so wide that all who chose might enter into practice, a broader privilege than is enjoyed, I believe, by any of the members of the mechanical fraternity. Other circumstances not now necessary to be enumerated strengthened their designs, and favored their deliberations, and there was no reason for delay. The auspicious hour had at length arrived, and the formation of an Academy of Medicine in this city was secured. This timely, this judicious, this important, this necessary movement, owed its creation to the wants and honor of the profession, and the perpetuity of its rights. Association, it was reasoned, would protect its claims as the noblest of pursuits, and its divine origin could not be abrogated by the statute book The year 1846 gave birth to the Academy; its incorporation was granted in 1852. I cannot now write the history of this successful institution during its first decennial. Our Nestors in Hippocratic science, moved by weighty reasons in behalf of public health and individual happiness, laid its foundation, and in this goodly work we find recorded the names of Stevens, Mott, Smith, Stewart, Wood, Reese, Kissam, Detmold, and Stearns.

The Academy has been generously fostered by an imposing number of the erudite and accomplished of the medical and surgical profession, and order and harmony have characterized all its proceedings. The subject-matter of discussion at its meetings, and the communications of its members, have had special interest, and have demonstrated that the faculty of close observation and acute reasoning is still among the diagnostic marks of the cultivated practical physician. Its printed transactions speak in louder accents of the excellence of its labors than my feeble pen can here express. With an inflexible intent to keep a watchful eye over the interests of professional learning and practical skill, to hold in reverential regard the obligations of sound medical ethics, to guard against the delusions and the medical heresies of the day, and at all times to cherish the rising merits of the junior associates in the art of healing, no apprehension need be felt that the Academy will prove otherwise than a rich boon to medical philosophy, and a blessing to this great, prosperous, and vastly increasing metropolis.

Like the Historical Society, the Academy of Medicine selected at its organization a venerable head as its first President, John Stearns. He had fulness of years, weight of character, and corresponding experience, and could look back with satisfaction on an extensive career of professional service. He was a native of Massachusetts, and born in 1770. He was graduated in the arts at Yale College in 1786. He attended the lectures of Rush, Shippen, Kuhn, and others of Philadelphia, but did not receive the doctorate until 1812, when the Regents of the University of New York conferred on him the honorary degree of M. D. He commenced the practical exercise of his profession at Waterford, afterwards at Albany and at Saratoga, and finally settled in the city of New York, where he maintained the reputation of an honorable, devoted, and benevolent physician, until the close of his long life, in March, 1848. His death, which was greatly lamented, was occasioned by a dissection wound, arising from his zeal to arrive, by a post-mortem examination, to more certain pathological conclusions, in a case of singular interest. He met this unexpected disaster with exemplary forbearance, and experienced the consolation of a Christian's hope in his final departure. The Academy paid appropriate funeral honors to his memory, and the Rev. Dr. Tyng, of St. George's Chapel, of which Dr. Stearns had long been a member, delivered an appropriate discourse on the life and character of the "Good Physician."

Great as was the devotion paid by Dr. Stearns to practical medicine, he was in earlier life enlisted in political affairs; and we find him in the Senate of the State of New York in 1812, and a member of the Council of Appointment. Shortly after the organization of the State Medical Society, he delivered the annual address, as President. He was for many years a Trustee of the College of Physicians and Surgeons. His name is recorded as one of the founders of the American Tract Society, and he took a deep interest in the welfare of the Bible Society, and the Institution for the benefit of the Deaf and Dumb. The annals of charity include his name in other institutions of a benevolent design. His philanthropic spirit cannot be questioned. His writings on the profession, and on subjects of a kindred nature, are scattered through the periodicals of the times. He is indissolubly associated with an heroic article of the materia medica, the virtues of which his clinical sagacity first brought to notice. His brief paper on Catalepsy attracted the attention of the learned Dr. Good. This short sketch must suffice to show that the Academy were judicious in their choice of their first officer, and both his inaugural address and the manner in which he fulfilled his trust, soon dismissed all doubt as to the wisdom of their suffrage. This venerable man gave dignity to the meetings; his courteousness secured deference and maintained authority; his knowledge and his impartiality added fairness to debate, and increased the gratification of intellectual association.

The office of President is filled by annual elections. The present head of the Academy is Valentine Mott, whose zeal and assiduity in behalf of the great interests of medical and surgical science, half a century's labors testify. The lustre of his great name seems to have still further swelled the number of friends to the Academy, and excited additional activity among them to promote the expressed designs of its incorporation.

When I subjected to manipulation the neglected philosopher, old Christopher Colles, the more advantageously to present him to the public view, I partially brought forward some occurrences which marked the literary condition of our metropolis. I design at present to enter a little more minutely into some circumstances associated with the advancement of knowledge in this city, particularly as connected with the time somewhat anterior to the establishment of the New York Historical Society, and then to notice a few prominent events of more recent date, which seem calculated to give confidence to the friends of intellectual rank, that the march of mind is a certain fact, and that we may look on with admiration at the achievements that have been already wrought, rather than cherish any despondency for the future. The trifling incidents with which I commence these literary memorials possess an intrinsic interest, inasmuch as they are decisive of the humble state and embarrassments in which instruction and knowledge generally were involved, and of the feeble powers which the Press, only two or three generations ago, sustained in this country. They are a suitable prelude to the great drama now enacting.

Southey has said that an American's first plaything is the rattlesnake's tail; and as he grows up he lays traps for opossums and shoots squirrels for his breakfast. This exaggeration may possibly have had a shadow of truth in it at the time when the pilgrim fathers established their first printing press, or when Bradford first published our laws, or even when the flying coach travelled once a week between New York and Philadelphia. An impartial examination of facts will generally lead to the conviction that elementary education for the most part accompanies the progress of population, and that the requirements of information are proportionably furnished. From her very commencement, it has seemed to me that New York has been characterized more by her scientific displays than by her literary products. The distinction which has been awarded her eminent men who have labored in the several liberal professions of law, physic, and divinity, would appear to justify the observation. Be this as it may, we have no difficulty in accounting for the absence of learning in our earlier days, when we contemplate the condition of the people at different epochs in their country's history, and weigh the force of circumstances; as for example, that in some instances where the Declaration of Independence being read at the head of military detachments, and then ordered to be printed for wider distribution, types could not be found to execute the work.

At the date at which I would commence these reminiscences, the old Daily Advertiser, and McLean's New York Gazette, were the leading oracles. The former, it is curious to observe, was printed with the press and types which had been used by Franklin in Philadelphia, and which, I am told, Poor Richard disposed of advantageously to Francis Childs, of New York. For mercantile purposes these papers did well, and had a corresponding circulation; they betokened in part the state of mental culture among the masses. If, however, we except the discussions on the American Constitution by the writers of the Federalist, and some few other subjects of national importance, by Rufus King, Noah Webster, Fisher Ames, and a few others, we may affirm that a single issue of some of our most popular papers of the present day, is enriched with more intellectual material than a year's file of these old journals. In 1793 was projected the Minerva, which under the control of its editor, Noah Webster, at once elevated the character of this species of periodical literature. Webster labored at this service some seven years, when the title of the paper was changed to that of the Commercial Advertiser, which has continued its diurnal course up to the present time, under the supervision of F. H. Hall, and has attained a longevity greater than that of any other journal ever originated in this city. The NewYork Magazine, projected by the Swords, was the only monthly periodical that received a becoming patronage, which sustained it for some eight or nine years, when it was succeeded by the American Magazine and the New York Review, whose writers were not unfrequently called the Mohawk reviewers, from their hostility to the rising Jacobinism of the times. The period of the existence of these periodicals was from 1790 to 1801. The first specified was the chosen vehicle for a series of essays of a literary circle, called the Drone Club. The association included many accomplished writers, Bleecker, Mitchill, Kent,

Miller, Wells, &c. The last survivor of the Drones was the late Chief Justice Samuel Jones, an early member of the Historical Society and a prodigy in black-letter learning. In 1797 the Medical Repository was commenced by Drs. Mitchill, Miller and Smith, the first journal of a scientific character the country could boast. The business of instruction in our preparatory schools was, with few exceptions, under the control of inadequate principals; in many instances the commonest business of life was abandoned on the demand for a teacher, and the responsible duties of an intellectual guide, undertaken by individuals whose chief recommendation was their dexterity with the awl and the hammer. Some qualified for the great trust, were, however, found. Edward Riggs, long the master of a grammar school in this city, published his Introduction to the Latin Tongue in 1784, the first indigenous work of that kind among us; and he was followed by James Hardy, the compiler of several compends for instruction in the classics, in 1793–'4. The remembrance of him is still vivid. He was an Aberdeen scholar; his early life was devoted to the seas; he became an inmate of the family of Dr. Beattie, who gave him recommendations as well qualified for a professorship of classical literature. At Dr. Beattie's suggestion he came out to this city. In his best estate he was an approved teacher. After a while he abandoned the schoolmaster's office, and finally sought a livelihood as a supernumerary of the Board of Health. He encountered the yellow fever in its most malignant form with consummate bravery during its several visitations after 1795, and compiled those volumes of facts and opinions on the pestilence which bear his name. He lived through many vicissitudes, and died of cholera, in 1832.

The elementary spelling books of Webster, and the geography of Morse, in my urchin days, were making their way to public approbation, not however without much opposition; they had a long contest with Dilworth and Salmon, and almost a score of years had passed before Pike and Root, authorities with the federal currency, overcame the schoolmaster's assistant and the Irishman Gough, with their sterling standard value of pounds, shillings and pence. Enfield's Speaker was forced to yield to Bingham's Preceptor, and Dwight's Columbia superseded Rule Britannia. I cannot dwell on the speculations thrown out by the teachers of the day on the merits and demerits of these instruments of their art, and on the necessity then urged by them, of a disenthralled and free nation exercising an independent judgment, with the patriotic endeavor to create a new literature for a regenerated people. With respect to books of practical science the same spirit was manifested, till at length we find at the commencement of this century, the New Practical Navigator of Nathaniel Bowditch, of Boston, securing its triumphs for every sea, over the time-honored Practical Navigator of Hamilton Moore, of Tower-hill, London.

This desire for fresh mental aliment under a new constitution was by no means limited; it spread far and wide, particularly in New England; it left, I believe, old Euclid unmolested, but it involved equally the infant primer and the elaborate treatise. In the colonial condition of affairs Sternhold and Hopkins had sustained many assaults, but their strongholds were now invaded by the popular zeal of Barlow and

Dwight. Nor were these innovations confined to sacred poetry alone. The psalmody which had for almost centuries mollified the distresses of the heart, and elevated the drooping spirits of the devout, surrendered its wonted claims to the Columbian Harmonist of Read. A tolerable library might be formed of the various productions of these operatives in the business of popular instruction. Noah Webster had engendered this zeal more perhaps than any other individual, and by incessant devotion had kept it alive. His Dissertations on the English Language he sent to Franklin, and Franklin in return wrote to Webster that his book would be useful in turning the thoughts of his countrymen to correct writing, yet administered to him profitable cautions. But literature, like the free soil of the country in these days, was infested with many weeds, and words ran high on many points of verbal logic. Amidst all these commotions some things were deemed too sacred on all sides to be molested. Such was the affecting history of the martyrdom of John Rodgers, burnt at Smithfield; but the nursery rhyme,

Whales in the sea—God's voice obey,

by acclamation was transformed into another equally undeniable truth:

By Washington—Great deeds were done.

A truth moreover which came home immediately to the feelings of the American bosom, and cleaved perhaps nearer the heart.

While the English language therefore, in the hands of the disciplinarians, was struggling for new powers and a loftier phraseology,—for few were enumerated in those days who believed with Gibbon and Franklin that the French tongue might absorb all other speech,—the patriotism of the youthful population ran no less wild than the literary ravings of the schoolmasters and the would-be philologists; yet as time has proved with like innocence to the detriment of the Republic. Wars and rumors of war kept the juveniles alive. Social companies of youngsters were formed, accoutred with wooden guns and kettle drums, and were perpetually seen, with braggart front in harmless squads, marching with the air of Capt. Bobadil, chanting some piece of continental poetry:

Behold! the conquering Yankees come
With sound of fife and beat of drum;
Says General Lee to General Howe,
What do you think of the Yankees now?

But these trifles were looked upon as the flying cloud; the nation had ripe men at its head; government was successfully securing the measures for commerce and finance; the schools were daily stronger with better teachers, and the halls of colleges were fuller supplied with candidates for elevated instruction. The press was more prolific, and something beside the Fool of Quality and Evelina, the Shepherd of Salisbury Plain and George Barnwell, were with the reading public. Pope, and Ann Radcliff, and Monk Lewis, might be found on the stalls, with Bonaparte's Campaigns in Italy. Franklin's life and essays were in everybody's hands. Dobson, of Philadelphia, had heroically undertaken the republication of the Encyclopædia Britannica, and Collins, of New Jersey, about the same time, had issued his highly prized quarto Family Bible. Nor were our New York publishers lukewarm at the printing of elaborate works of grave import and scholastic value. If, however, we except the Poems of Freneau and the reprint of Burns, we find little in the region of the muses that issued from the press; Clifton, Honeywood, Low, and Linn, were our prominent domestic poets.

The Della Cruscan muse now, however, invaded us: Mrs. Robinson's Poems was a dog-eared volume; and the song of the melodious Bard, Rogers, "I knew by the smoke that so gracefully curled," received a popularity surpassing that of perhaps any other verses. It found its way in the daily journals, weekly museums, weekly visitors and ladies' magazines; it was printed on single sheets, placarded at inns and in stage coaches; it travelled to the races as the inner lining of hats; it occupied the cabins of the wood boats, and was found surrounding the trunk of the orchard tree; it was among the earliest of our music printing, and old Dr. Anderson, now some eighty years of age, our first engraver on wood, still alive and still busy, gave it illustrations; it was seen among the contents of the young misses' reticule, and was read in secret at the doors of churches, while the youthful maiden was tarrying for a partner to accompany her within the house of worship. My defective memory does not permit me to state positively that Blanchard, in his aeronautic expeditions, wafted it to the skies. In short, it was everywhere. But the prospects of a French war and Hail Columbia ere long limited the duration of this electric poem; and as if to facilitate this object, here and there appeared a sylvan rhymist who entwined a chaplet of the Rosa Matilda order. What had been considered rare, now lost its freshness, and spurious articles had currency in the market without detection by the multitude. The pretensions of the Della Cruscan finery came at last to a somewhat sudden and unexpected end in the humorous effusion of Barrett:

> "If all the geese in Lincoln fens
> Produced spontaneous well-made pens;
> If Red Sea, Black Sea, White Sea ran
> One tide of ink to Ispahan;
> Had I the stenographic power
> To write ten libraries in an hour,
> 'T were all in vain to paint the grace
> Of half a freckle on thy face."

One or two additional circumstances may be stated to strengthen what has already been said, rather than create doubt as to the accuracy of our narrative. Campbell and Bloomfield appeared as authors in London with little interval between them. The Pleasures of Hope and the Farmer's Boy were here reprinted nearly simultaneously; the former had been subjected to the revision of Dr. Anderson, the editor of the British Poets; the latter had undergone the incubation of Capel Lofft. Thus fortified, there was little hesitation as to the safety of the undertaking. Such was the importance attached to these works, that the rival publishers blazened forth their labors, so that every corner of the city was enlivened by large placards announcing the important fact. It is almost superfluous to add, that with the literary taste which had been cherished, the Farmer's Boy outran in popularity the Pleasures of Hope. As the case now stands, Campbell makes one of every dozen volumes we meet with, while it might be difficult to find a copy of Bloomfield.

In 1804 Scott enriched the poetic world with his Lay of the Last Minstrel. Soon after its appearance a presentation copy of the work in luxurious quarto was received by a lady, then a resident of this city, a native of Scotland, and who had been most intimate with the author when school companions in the same institution. It was seen that the Minstrel was a classic, and the volume circulated widely among friends. It shortly after fell into the hands of a publishing house, and the great question now to be decided was, whether it could bear an American reprint, keeping in view the primary object of the bookseller, that the wheel of fortune must turn in the right way. A literary coterie was selected who might determine the chances of adventure. Among other dissuasive arguments, the Lay was pronounced too local in its nature, and its interest obsolete; its measure was considered too varied and irregular, and it had not the harmony of tuneful Pope. It was rejected by the critical tribunal. Longworth, however, brought sufficient resolution to bear, and printed in his Belles-Lettres Repository of 1805, the universally known introduction to the first canto. Such was the cool and calculating reception of Scott with us. One might almost think from the opening lines of the poem, that the poet had, with prophetic vision, foreseen himself in the New World:

> "The way was long, the night was cold,
> The Minstrel was infirm and old."

These were probably the first lines of Walter Scott's writings that ever issued from an American press. The memorable quarto is still preserved with many associations by the venerable lady to whom the illustrious author presented it, Mrs. Divie Bethune, the founder of our Infant schools. Who can now tell the hundreds of thousands of volumes of this noble writer which the press of this country has brought forth?

We are not to be abashed at the recital of these occurrences concerning the early condition of the press. They were associated, and naturally grew out of the spirit of the times and the condition of the Republic. Scott was a new name among authors, and elegant letters are not among the first wants of a people. Yet it will be conceded that at that very period a broad foundation was already being laid, on which at no remote day literature, as well as science, would command its disciples. The trepidation at the hazard of printing a few leaves of poetry experienced by some, is to be judged merely as an individual infirmity, inasmuch as we find that even then typography was prolific of works of voluminous extent, and many of its products at that day constitute a sound portion of existing libraries. Longworth himself was a man of enterprise, but he had bought experience by his ornamental edition of Hayley's Triumphs of Temper, and he was moreover sustaining his Shakspeare Gallery at no small sacrifice; while we find that Evert Duyckinck, Isaac Collins, George F. Hopkins, Samuel Campbell, and T. and J. Swords, were the leading men to whom we may turn for evidence that the press was not idle, and for illustration of the rising capabilities of the book-publishers' craft. An author was a scarce article in those days, about the beginning of the nineteenth century; the returns for literary labor must have been small. Noah Webster was unquestionably the most successful of the tribe, and in his wake followed the geographer Morse. The city library, and the circulating library of Caritat, constituted pretty much all the establishments of that order we possessed. Pintard was then at New Orleans, and years elapsed before he and the excellent William Wood began to think of the Apprentices' Library, and to suggest the Mariners' Library for ships at sea. The Mercantile Library, now so vast a concern, was not then dreamt of, and Philip Hone, with all his ardor as a patriotic citizen, had not as yet enlisted in the great cause of knowledge, or manifested that attention to those important interests which absorbed the years of his more advanced life. In a pedestrian excursion through our then thinly populated streets, one might see the ample Dr. Mitchill and his colleague Dr. Miller, Dr. Bayley, Dr. Hosack, Dr. S. Miller, Dr. Mason, and Dunlap, all writers; Caines, the deep-read reporter; Cheetham and Coleman, the antagonistic editors; and Kent, afterwards the great Chancellor. In the court room we might behold Hamilton and Burr, Brockholst Livingston and Martin Wilkins, Colden and Slosson, Hoffman and Pendleton, and young Wells.*

* To render these imperfect sketches of the times less defective, I had designed to notice briefly the New York Bar, with which I was partially acquainted, by my repeated visits at the courts; often as medical witness in behalf of the people in criminal cases involving medical jurisprudence; but my resources are not adequate to the great subject, and the undertaking is the less necessary after the precious and interesting History of the Court of Common Pleas, from the pen of the Hon. Charles F. Daly, one of the Judges, and printed in volume 1st of the Reports of Cases, by Counsellor E. Delafield Smith. Some forty-five years ago, my lamented friend and associate of Columbia College, Samuel Berrian, brother of the venerable Rector of Trinity Church, commenced a series of Sketches of the Members of the Bar, which appeared in Dennie's Portfolio. His first subject was Josiah Ogden Hoffman, with whom he was a pupil. The great men of the legal profession of those days to which I allude, were indeed by universal concurrence, enumerated among the master minds of the land; and I have often heard it said, that the voice of the law, from their

The literary struggles of those days deserve more ample notice, but our task may be honestly abridged at this time. The curious in a knowledge of literary toil, in the progress of letters, and in the details of authorship, will not fail frequent consultation of the several works of the late Dr. Griswold, a faithful pioneer of mental acumen in this department of study, and turn with renewed delight and increased satisfaction to the Biographical Essays of the æsthetic Tuckerman, and the pages of the Cyclopædia of American Literature, by the Messrs. Duyckinck. When thoroughly investigated, the candid inquirer may wonder that under such difficulties so much was in reality accomplished.

So long ago as in 1802 I had the pleasure of witnessing the first social gathering of American publishers at the old City Hotel, Broadway, an organization under the auspices of the venerable Matthew Carey. About thirty years after I was one of a large assembly brought together by the Brothers Harper's great entertainment. I remember well the literary wares displayed on that

lips, was the harmony of the world. Legal medicine, I am inclined to think, received more homage in the days of Thomas Addis Emmet and Hugh Maxwell, the District Attorney, than it had before or has since. Emmet was profoundly learned as a physician; in all cases of death that came before him requiring medical testimony, an examination of the brain he made a prerequisite. It is not irrelevant to add, that Dr. James S. Stringham is to be considered the founder of Medical Jurisprudence in this country. He was the first who gave lectures on this science in America, and was my predecessor in the chair of Forensic Medicine in the University of New York. His taste for this knowledge he originally imbibed from his able preceptor, Dr. Duncan, of Edinburgh. His reading on the subject was extensive, from the elaborate investigations of Paulus Zacchias, down to the recent productions of Foderè and Mahon. A fuller account of him may be found in my Sketch, in Beck's Medical Jurisprudence. He was a native of New York, and died in 1817.

first memorable occasion, and I still see in "my mind's eye" the prominent group of American authors who participated in the festivities of the latter celebration. Again in 1855 a complimentary festival of the New York Book Publishers' Association to authors and booksellers took place at the Crystal Palace. A comparative view of these three periods in literary progress would furnish an instructive illustration of the workings of the American mind and of the enterprise and capabilities of the American press. The venerable Matthew Carey at the primary meeting held forth, in earnest language, persuasives to renewed meetings of a like nature as the most effective means for the promotion and diffusion of knowledge. Isaac Collins, that jewel of a man for solid worth and integrity, concurred in sentiment. At the Harper entertainment similar opinions proceeded from many minds, and the liveliest responses in confirmation were listened to from Chancellor Kent and a large number of native writers of celebrity. At the last celebration of 1855, which was conducted on a scale of great variety and elegance, Washington Irving and a most imposing association of distinguished authors, male and female, graced the occasion: those public spirited publishers, the Appletons, with Wiley and Putnam, rendered the banquet a genial gathering of kindred spirits. The intelligent and patriotic Putnam, in an appropriate introductory address, stated the fact that for twelve years, ending in 1842, there were published 1,115 different works, of these 623 were original; in the year 1853 there were 733 new works published in the United States, of which 276 were reprints of English works, 35 were translations of foreign authors, and 420 original American works; thus showing an increase of about 800 per cent. in less than twenty years. Mr. Putnam thus draws the conclusion that literature and the book-trade advanced ten times as fast as the population. If with these facts we compare the numbers printed of each edition, the growth is still greater: editions at the present time varying from 10,000, 30,000, 75,000, and even 300,000. The Magazine of the Messrs. Harper reaches the astounding number at each issue of 180,000. On this last memorable occasion of the publishers' celebration our distinguished poet, Bryant, responded to a sentiment on American literature in his happiest manner. I quote a few lines from his suggestive address: "The promise of American authorship, given by the appearance of Cotton Mather, has never been redeemed till now. In him the age saw one of its ripest scholars, though formed in the New England schools and by New England libraries, in the very infancy of the colonies; a man, as learned as the author of the Anatomy of Melancholy, and sometimes as quaintly eloquent, sending out huge quartos as the fruit of his labors, interspersed with duodecimos, the fruit of his recreations; but his publications exceeded the number of the days of the year. After his time, in the hundred and fifty years which followed, the procession of American authors was a straggling one; at present they are a crowd which fairly choke the way; illustrious historians, able and acute theologians, authors of books of travels, instructive or amusing, clever novelists, brilliant essayists, learned and patient lexicographers. Every bush, I had almost said every buttercup of the fields has its poet; poets start up like the soldiers of Roderick Dhu, from behind every rock and out of every bank of fern."

I must linger a moment longer on this subject. Our literary annals, while they abound with occurrences most gratifying to the intellectual and moral advancement of our species, possess yet another claim to estimation. The making of books has not been an employment of selfish and inert gratification; it has proved a prolific source of emolument, no less remarkable than the peculiar occasions which have awakened the talents necessary for the healthy exercise of the art itself. Literature, independently of its own noble nature, has superadded to its powers a productive result of substantial issue; and while it beautifies and enriches with precious benefits the progress of civilization, it has secured the comforts which spring up from the wholesome pursuit of other sources of wealth. This indeed is the offspring of but a recent period among us; but the fact is not the less solacing to the pangs of intellectual labor. The huckstering which once marred the transactions between publishers and authors no longer occurs; the starveling writers whom I now and then saw, at about the time of the first meeting of our literary venders, the booksellers of 1802, have paid the debt of nature, I dare not add prematurely; and we can now enroll a list of the literary and the scientific who have increased far and wide the nation's renown. For a considerable while during my early medical career my diagnosis often led me to attribute the causes of mental inquietude and physical suffering among this circumscribed order of men to inanition; but if the literary squad, as old Dr. Tillary denominated them, preserve intact their wonted energies and privileges, their improved condition may sometimes demand an alterative treatment corresponding with that robust state and imposing plethora, in which they so generally present themselves to our admiration and esteem. Personal observation and individual experience may have helped the great reform, for not a few must have learned the truth of the remark of the playwright, George Colman: "Authorship, as a profession, is a very good walking-stick, but very bad crutches." For this salutary change in the Republic of Letters let all praise be given to knowledge more available, to the higher culture of the people, and to the patronage of our enlightened publishers. I allude to such authors as Irving, Cooper, Bancroft, Taylor, Bryant, Halleck, and Paulding, and refer to such patrons as the Appletons, the Harpers, Scribner, Wiley and Putnam. I am limited to New York in these specifications. Let Sparks and Prescott, Ticknor, Longfellow, Holmes, Hawthorne and Everett speak of their Boston literary firms. What Childs and Peterson have done for the generous enterprise of the lamented Kane, both in the mechanical execution of those endearing volumes, the Arctic Expedition, and in the returns secured by liberal appropriation in artistic display, is enough of itself for the renown of Philadelphia. Nor can I omit to notice in this connection, that the most complete and authentic Dictionary of Authors in our vernacular tongue is in progress of publication under the auspices of this enterprising house, for which noble monument of literary toil and industry we are indebted to the accomplished S. A. Allibone, of Philadelphia; while in our own city, we are promised by D. Appleton & Co., ere long, a New Cyclopædia of General Knowledge, especially rich in native science and biography, prepared by the erudite and gifted editors, George Ripley and Charles A. Dana.

I believe I have secured the concurrence of my audience in the opinion that I have already said enough of the eventful Past in its complex relations with the New York Historical Society. If I mistake not, the narrative which I have given of the passing events and living movements of our times elucidates the incalculable value of your Institution, and points out how indispensable is the duty to cherish that conservative element which your charter demands. The fragmentary information brought together in this discourse may not be wholly without its use: it may serve at least to furnish some hints to subsequent writers who may venture to fill up, with higher aspirations, the mighty void which exists in the annals of this vast Metropolis. With the philosophical historian every new fact will be duly appreciated, the transitory nature of many occurrences better understood in their relation to simultaneous events, and the men of consequence in their day more faithfully estimated. Skill indeed will be demanded in selection and judgment in arrangement, but an enlarged vision will comprehend the truth that what seems temporary may sometimes become permanent, that what is local often becomes national.

The task assigned me by your courtesy for this day's celebration has been executed amidst many cares, and not without apprehensions as to the result. The moments seized for preparation have not always been the most auspicious; but my native feelings and my love of the olden times, have prompted the spirit and the tendency of this address. " Whatever," says the great moralist, Dr. Johnson, " makes the past, the distant, and the future predominate over the present, exalts us in the scale of thinking beings." None can feel more deeply than myself the imperfect execution of the service I have attempted, and none of its deficiencies causes greater uneasiness than the circumstance that I have omitted notice of many of the eminent dead whose names ought to be placed on a record of gratitude, for their labors in behalf of this society in its earlier existence. While I am conscious that the men of to-day are not inferior to those whose rank they now supply, I have also been compelled to overlook a long catalogue of living worthies, who still co-operate in the great design of rearing this Historical Institution to national consideration. Fortunately your printed Collections and Proceedings, a long series, have perpetuated the contributions of many of these distinguished members, and posterity will seek instruction and delight in the discourses which you have preserved of your Clinton and Verplanck, your Morris and Hosack, your Mitchill and Blunt, your Wheaton and Lawrence, your Kent and Butler, your Bradford and Bancroft. The records of your secretary will point out your indebtedncss to those long tried members who have adhered to your interests in seasons of greatest depression; Chancellor Matthews, the founder, I may add, of our City University; George B. Rapelye, a friend with a Knickerbocker's heart, who has often invigorated my statements by his minute knowledge; Samuel Ward, a generous benefactor to your rich possessions, and Albert Gallatin, many years your presiding officer, who needs no voucher of mine to place him in the front rank of intellectual mortals.

The thousand and one occurrences which have weighed on my mind while in this attempt to sketch a picture of the times in New York during the past sixty years, have made the difficulty of choice perplexing to recollection and embarrassing to the judgment. It might have been more acceptable to many had this Discourse been concentrated on some special topics of general interest, or that the importance of history as a philosophical study had been set forth, the better to urge the high claims which this institution proffers to the countenance and support of this enlightened community. I stand amenable to such criticism, yet I fain would trust that the leaves of memory which I have opened may not be altogether without their use. An indifferent observer of the events of so long a period in a city of such progress, could not fail to have arrived at a knowledge of many things characteristic of the age and profitable as practical wisdom; to one who has ever cherished a deep sympathy in whatever adds to the renown of the city of his birth, or increases the benefits of its population, the accumulation of facts would naturally become almost formidable; and while with becoming deference his aim on such an occasion as the present would lead him in his selection to group together, without tedious minuteness, the more prominent incidents which have marked its career, it might be tolerated if he here and there, with fond reluctance, dwelt upon what most involved his feelings, even should the subject-matter prove inefficient in popular importance. In the wide and fertile field which I have entered, it required an anthologist of rare gifts to select with wisdom products the healthiest, the richest, and most grateful for general acceptance, and most conducive to the general design.

The inquiry may be fairly put, has the New York Historical Society stood an isolated institution during its long career, and are its merits of an exclusive character? It may be promptly answered, No: It was preceded in its formation by the Massachusetts Historical Society, a bright example for imitation, some ten or twelve years; and it has been followed by the organization of many other historical societies formed in different and widely-distant states of the Union. They have grown up around her, not by the desire of imitation, but by the force of utility, and I will be bold enough to affirm, that consultation of their numerous volumes is indispensable to an author who aims at writing a faithful local or general history of the country. I speak thus earnestly because I think these works are too much overlooked or neglected. The conjoint labors of these several associations, with commendable diligence, are securing for future research, authentic materials touching events in history, in the arts, in science, in jurisprudence, and in literature; and if I mistake not, the intelligence of the people is awakened to their import; individual pride and state ambition have been invoked in furtherance of the measure, and results productive of national good must crown the efforts. Truth, it is often said, is reserved for posterity—truth promulgated may be doubly fortified by these historical societies.

In the march of similar pursuits, we may notice the American Antiquarian Society, founded by the late Isaiah Thomas, and the New England Historical and Genealogical Society, a recent organization, whose labors however already amount to many volumes, aided by the herculean devotion of Samuel G. Drake, and the still more recent Historical Magazine published by Richardson, of Boston. This last-named periodical gives promise of excellence of the highest order.

I would call attention to our New York Ethnological Society, now founded several years. Its volumes which have met the eye, evince that the Association has adepts among its members able to throw light on the most intricate subjects of human inquiry. Its present president is the learned Dr. Robinson, so distinguished in philology and biblical literature.

Still more recently a Geographical Society has sprung up among us. Though of but short duration, its transactions have commanded approbation both abroad and at home. Among its leading members is Henry Grinnell, the well-known promoter of the Arctic expeditions under the direction of Captain Kane. The Rev. Dr. Hawks, the archæologist, is the present head of this association.

As connected with the great design of promoting useful knowledge, the institution of the Lyceum of Natural History in this city may be included in the number. This association has now been in operation forty years. It was founded by Mitchill in union with Dr. Torrey, the late Dr. Townsend, and a few others. The Lyceum is most strictly devoted to natural history; it created an early impulse to studies illustrative of our natural products in the several kingdoms of nature, and it is familiarly recognized for its novel and able contributions. Many of the rarest treasures of our marine waters have become known by the investigations of the Lyceum: among its scientific supporters, are Torrey, De Kay, Cooper, Le Conte, and Jay. Like the Academy of Natural Sciences of Philadelphia, the Boston Natural History Society, and the Society of Charleston, S. C., with its President Holbrook, its opinions are authoritative.

The impulse given to intellectual labor in these, our own times, is still further shown in the completion of that great undertaking, the Natural History of the State of New York. This vast project was, I believe, commenced during the administration of Governor Seward, and if we value science by the research which it displays, this extensive work presents claims of unquestionable excellence to our recognition. Its able authors, with a scrutinizing observation that has never tired, have unfolded the richness of our native productions to the delight of the naturalist and to the cultivators of our domestic resources. The work is a lasting memorial of the public spirit of the state, and an index to the legislative wisdom of its rulers. The felicitous introduction to the entire series of volumes from the pen of Governor Seward, will always be perused with emotions of patriotic pride. Associated with another measure not less public spirited, is the Documentary History of the State of New York, under the direction of executive authority, and prepared for the press by the editorial supervision of Dr. O'Callaghan. Its importance cannot be over-estimated; and the judgment displayed in the disposition of its multifarious materials, increases the desire that no impediment may arrest the completion of a miscellany of knowledge hitherto inaccessible. Less could not be said of the labors of Dr. O'Callaghan, when we remember that these documents include the Brodhead Papers.

Is it speaking too earnestly, when it is said that the Republic at large appears determined to secure her history from doubt and uncertainty? Associations for the preservation of historical materials seem springing up in every state. We find them in the north and in the south, in the east and in the west; and have learned that religious denominations are engaged in like duties, to secure authentic records of the trials and progress of their respective creeds. In our own city the Baptists have formed an historical society, at the head of which is the venerable David T. Valentine, the editor of the Corporation Manual, which yearly enlarges our topographical and civil history; and an association of the Protestant Episcopal faith has recently published two volumes of Historical Records in illustration of the early condition of the Church. All this looks well, and I am confident that our association contemplates with pleasurable emotions these rival efforts in so good a cause.

The New York Historical Society has work enough for her strongest energies to accomplish. The state under whose auspices she flourishes, is indeed an empire; the transactions which claim her consideration possess an inherent greatness, and are momentous in their nature; her colonial career is pregnant with instructive events; the advances she has made, and the condition she has secured in her state policy, afford lessons which the wisest may study with profit. Long neglect has only increased the duty of investigation, and added value to every new revelation offered. The Hudson and Niagara are but types of her physical formation. Her geology has dissolved the theories of the closet, and given new principles to geognostic science. Her men of action have been signally neglected. Feeble records only are to be found of her most eminent statesmen. Where shall we look, throughout our country's annals, for a more heroic spirit, one of more personal courage, of greater devotion to his country, one greater in greatest trial, one of more decision of character, one of sterner integrity, than Gov. George Clinton, to whom this State and the Union are under such mighty obligations; and yet we fruitlessly search for a worthy memorial of him. Fellow associates, I repeat it, there is work enough to do.

I have spoken of history and its many relations. History the schoolmen have divided into sacred and profane. All history may be deemed sacred, inasmuch as it teaches the ways of God, whose eternity knows neither time nor space, and unfolds the anatomy of that microcosm man, the image of his Maker. History is a deep philosophy, yet capable of appropriation to vulgar designs; it is a prodigious monitor, a mighty instructor. Be it our aim to use it for beneficent ends, cherishing as a rule of life the revealed truth, that there is a still higher wisdom within our reach, and that our intelligence, however great, must recognize the inflexible sentence, uttered of old; the tree of knowledge is not the tree of life.

*Mr. President:*

For a series of years you have held the elevated office of head of the Historical Society. The distinguished men, your predecessors, who have filled that prominent station, have, I believe, all departed. You stand the sole representative of a long list of worthies who have discharged trusts similar to those committed to you, and which your wisdom and experience in public councils and in state affairs have enabled you to fortify with an ability which reflects credit on your administration, and has proved signally advantageous to this institution. The duties which have devolved on you may at times have been onerous, but if I can fathom your nature, must have proved grateful to your feelings, and congenial to your patriotism. Your copious reading had made you familiar with the great events of the two wars, which this state waged, and in which she was so great a sufferer, but in which she proved successful: more valuable materials, growing out of such circumstances, for the future historian could not be gathered from any other colony. This society, amidst its other treasures, has secured for the most part these precious documents; and from the period at which New York assumed the sovereignty of an independent State, there are few intervals pregnant with important events the records of which are not to be found in our archives. Thus, Sir, if ever an association adhered with fidelity to a literal interpretation of its charter power, it may be affirmed to be that in whose transactions you have taken so deep an interest. The work demanded intelligence, and it received it; it called for devotion and earnestness, and they were at hand; and thus was secured that continuity of effort so requisite to accomplish the undertaking. With what judgment the work has been executed, must be left to the decision of our arbiters, the public; I fear not the verdict.

Scholarship, the learned have said, was a rare acquisition in England, until the time of Bentley. It may as truthfully be asserted, that until the career of our founder commenced, there was little antiquarian zeal among us; and hence you may have perceived, that on several occasions I have ventured to place JOHN PINTARD in the foremost ground in the picture. The head and the heart of our eastern brethren exercise a warmer devotion for knowledge of this nature, than is found elsewhere in our Union; and the rare example on that account of my old friend proffered its claims to my notice in strongest accents. Let me say, Sir, that the forerunner in the course you so triumphantly have maintained, was not a mere holiday officer, but an untiring laborer in the great design. The talent he possessed was of peculiar value, and under certain circumstances might have commanded the highest premium. He had a fitness for the work, and none can rob him of the honor.

Your able Vice-Presidents have, I believe, concurred with you, at all times, in furtherance of those enlarged plans and that policy, which, as occasion demanded, have proved most salutary to the institution. Their enlightened coöperation must, on some occasions, have lessened individual responsibility, and lightened perplexities in the path of duty. I am inclined to think, that there is an unity of opinion throughout the society in commendation of the manner in which the various services, rendered by your fiscal and other committees, your secretaries, corresponding and recording, have been discharged. In times like these, sagacity in finance may be acknowledged wisdom of the highest order; and the fruits of sound forethought, when demonstrated by palpable results, yield arguments that cannot be demolished. I have but to add, that your intelligent and indefatigable librarian has nobly fulfilled his accountable appointment. Every thing around me leads to the conviction that your literary treasures have been preserved; your MS. records regarded at a proper estimate; your library so disposed, that every accommodation can be given to the searcher after wisdom in this curious repository of historical material.

Where all deserve commendation, and there remains nothing for censure, conscious rectitude yields unadulterated satisfaction to official capacity.

Mr. President: An abiding conviction prevails, that the interests of the society have been in proper hands, and controlled by wise councils. The memory of your administration will long endure with us. The ornamental and stately edifice, in which we are now gathered, erected by the liberality of our citizens, and in an especial manner by that class so often found generous in good works, the mercantile community, will, I trust, stand, for generations to come, a monument of the public spirit of New York—of her love and devotion to the refined and useful—and vindicate to the rising youth of the nation the estimate which their fathers formed of the blessings of wisdom derived from pure historical truth. If I am rightly informed, I stand before you, at this Anniversary, the oldest living member of this association. Yet have I consoled myself with the pleasing thought, while meditating on the eventful occurrences of this day, that although the sun of my declining years is nearly set, its last rays, however feeble, are reflected from the classical walls of the New York Historical Society.

FINIS.

# PROCEEDINGS

OF THE

# NEW YORK HISTORICAL SOCIETY,

AT THE

# DEDICATION OF THE LIBRARY,

TUESDAY, NOVEMBER 3, 1857.

NEW YORK:
PRINTED FOR THE SOCIETY.
M DCCC LVII.

# Officers of the Society, 1857.

PRESIDENT,
LUTHER BRADISH.

FIRST VICE-PRESIDENT,
THOMAS DE WITT, D.D.

SECOND VICE-PRESIDENT,
FREDERIC DE PEYSTER.

FOREIGN CORRESPONDING SECRETARY,
EDWARD ROBINSON, D.D.

DOMESTIC CORRESPONDING SECRETARY,
SAMUEL OSGOOD, D.D.

RECORDING SECRETARY,
ANDREW WARNER.

TREASURER,
WILLIAM CHAUNCEY.

LIBRARIAN,
GEORGE HENRY MOORE.

---

## Executive Committee.

AUGUSTUS SCHELL, CHAIRMAN.
MARSHALL S. BIDWELL.
BENJAMIN H. FIELD.
FRANCIS L. HAWKS, D.D.
JOHN ROMEYN BRODHEAD.
ERASTUS C. BENEDICT.
BENJ. ROBERT WINTHROP.

---

Secretary of the Executive Committee,
GEORGE HENRY MOORE.

# New York Historical Society.

# DEDICATION OF THE LIBRARY,

NOVEMBER 3, 1857.

THE Society assembled in the Lecture Room, at the usual hour. As the evening was devoted to the dedication of the building, by ceremonies directed to be observed by the Committee of Arrangements appointed at a previous meeting, the ordinary business was dispensed with, except the report of the Executive Committee on nominations, and nominations of new members.

Prayer was then offered by the Rev. THOMAS DE WITT, D. D., First Vice President of the Society.

The Hon. LUTHER BRADISH, President, then addressed the Society, as follows:

### ADDRESS OF THE PRESIDENT.

We are at length assembled for the first time under our own roof. The New York Historical Society has passed its nomadic state, and has at last found a fixed and permanent home. From wandering for half a century, the tenants at will of others, we come this evening to take possession, as our own, of this beautiful temple, with all its ample accommodations, and to dedicate them to the cause of history and of art

—of history in its broadest sense, and of art in its illustrations of history.

Here, for the benefit of the present and future generations, will history garner up its treasures. Here will each succeeding age, for the instruction of those to come after it, bring its record of the current events of time. And here, too, in the future, will the Genius of History from these accumulated treasures, construct its variegated but harmonious narrative—showing the relations and dependencies of apparently isolated events, and exhibiting the great truth that the histories of seemingly detached periods, instead of forming integral subjects complete in themselves, are but parts of the universal system of that Providence which, in infinite intelligence and wisdom, governs the world.

Here, too, in this fitting temple, will art lend the light and the fascination of its illustrations to the great truths of history. The genius which inspired the imagination and guided the pencil of Raphael, of Michael Angelo, of Rubens, and of Murillo, will hereafter cover these walls with its beautiful creations, illustrative of the men, the manners, and the events of the time ; and prove to mankind that in art the present is not inferior to the past, or the New World to the Old.

Sculpture, too, whose magic power can call from the inert and shapeless mass the ideal semblance of animated and intellectual life, even in its sublimest forms ; which can give to marble, in the graceful lineaments of female form and loveliness its chisel traces, the combined expression of the shrinking delicacy of female modesty and the force and dignity of conscious virtue ; which, in its magical transformations, can exhibit, in the quarried block, the first dawn of civilization, and the first springing of celestial hope in the bosom of a graceful daughter of the forest ; or can in marble symbolize the ethereal spirit's flight from darkness into light, and from time to eternity—this noble art will hereafter adorn these galleries with the productions of its genius, and prove to the world that America, too, can furnish names worthy to be associated with those of Thorwaldsen and Canova, of Phidias and Praxiteles.

The burin of the engraver, too, will lend its aid to enrich our galleries, and in its representations of both painting and sculpture, exhibit the magic of light and shade, the grace of outline and the beauty of design. Thus will these several departments of art conspire to illustrate and give additional interest to the truths of history, and thereby advance the proper objects of this society.

Ten years have passed away since the project of this building first received a definite form. In 1847 the New York Historical Society, then comparatively few in numbers, and feeble in pecuniary resources, but deeply impressed with the great and increasing value of its library and collections, and with the danger to which they were exposed, took the incipient steps for the erection of a new fire-proof edifice, for the reception and preservation of that library and those collections, and for the general accommodation of the Society. This enterprise, under the circumstances, might well, as it did, to the timid and even prudent, seem hardy. It was indeed bold. For the Society resolved upon an undertaking of great magnitude and importance, involving a large expenditure of money, without having in its treasury a single dollar for its achievement. But the Society relied upon the intelligence and known liberality of New York, in the confident belief that her public spirit would not permit an object of such conceded merit, and of so great public concernment, to fail for want of the necessary means for its accomplishment. It was, therefore, determined that an appeal, accompanied by a statement of facts, should be made to the public generally, and to the friends of historical literature in particular, for aid in the accomplishment of this great object of general interest. Most nobly did the public of New York respond to this appeal, and by its liberality and public spirit in promptly furnishing the requisite pecuniary means, fully justify the confidence of the Society and the wisdom of its enterprise. To collect and apply those means, however, has required a long time, great effort, and continued perseverance. But the success which has at length crowned persevering effort, should render us insensible to the exertions which have achieved that success; and, in the important good thus accomplished, we should forget the personal sacrifices it has cost and regard only the new hopes it inspires, and the increased responsibilities it involves.

On the 17th of October, 1855, this enterprise, thus commenced, had progressed with such encouraging success, that the corner stone of the present building was laid, and the work thenceforward steadily advanced. That liberality and public spirit which were so nobly manifested at the inception of this enterprise, still accompanied its continued prosecution, until, in this finished and beautiful structure, you now behold the consummation of an enterprise commenced in weakness, but in hope, perseveringly prosecuted in anxiety and with great effort, and at length crowned with ample and entire success. The two cardinal conditions, also, upon which this enterprise was undertaken, have been faithfully observed, and are this evening fulfilled. This new edifice was to be fire-proof. It is substantially so; and, when completed, no debt was to remain upon the Society on account of it. This, also, is true. The report of the Trustees of the Building Fund, which will be presented to you in the course of the evening, will, among other interesting details, announce the gratifying fact that, after faithfully discharging every just obligation incurred in procuring the site, and in the erection of this new fire-proof edifice, there will still remain, on account of this special fund, a balance to go towards the furnishing of the building for the uses of the Society. The further sum required to complete the payments for the necessary furniture of the building, alone now remains to be provided for. A voluntary contribution of a very few dollars from each member of the Society would abundantly supply the deficiency, and fully accomplish the desired object of finally closing this great enterprise. This small sum would in each case bear but a very inconsiderable proportion to the greatly increased accommodations and advantages procured to each member of the Society by the very satisfactory completion of this enterprise. Thus the two original and important conditions of this enterprise are this evening fulfilled. Your building is essentially fire-proof, and there will remain upon the Society, on account of it and its site, no debt, except, indeed, one of deep gratitude to those munificent patrons of the enterprise who have generously furnished the means of its accomplishment. To those generous patrons we point to this new and beautiful structure as an enduring and fit monument to their own liberality and public spirit. To the Society generally who originally projected and undertook this enterprise, and has watched with the deepest interest its progress and its completion, we present this noble edifice, with all its tasteful arrangements, its ample accommodations, and its admirable adaptation to its objects, as the reward of its enterprise, its perseverance and its ultimate and complete success.

With the successful accomplishment of this enterprise, a new and brighter era in the history of this Society is inaugurated. With these enlarged accommodations, and these greatly increased facilities, for the prosecution and accomplishment of its objects, the responsibilities of the Society are correspondingly increased. In proportion, as its library and collections are rendered more safe and more available, will be the inducement and the obligations of the Society to extend the former and enlarge the latter.

That these new and increased responsibilities will, in the future, be fully and honorably met by the Society, we have an assurance in its past history. But, for the ability to meet in a fit and becoming manner these new and increased responsibilities by increased activity, enlarged operations, and more extended usefulness, we must still look to the continued encouragement and patronage of that generous public which smiled so benignly upon the infancy of the Society; which has so generously fostered its youth, and which surely will not withhold from its ripening manhood the encouragement it may hereafter need, and shall deserve. Let it then be our object as a society fully to merit the patronage we seek. Let us, in entering upon the new and more brilliant career now opened before us, go forward with new energy and increased zeal; and, by judicious administration and greater activity in our operations, justify the appeals made to the public in our behalf, giving back to that public the cultivated fruits of its own munificence; and thus rendering this Society what, if wisely conducted, it cannot fail to be—both an ornament and a blessing to New York and our country.

Frederic de Peyster, Esq., Chairman of the Trustees of the Building Fund, submitted and read a report from that body.

REPORT.

*To the New York Historical Society:*

The doubts and anxieties of the past have vanished, and the expectations of the Trustees, and, may they hope, of the Society, are realized by the accomplishment of the work committed to their charge. You have this evening met to dedicate this spacious edifice to the important and deeply interesting objects, for the promotion of which this Society was organized. Upwards of a half century has passed away since a few public-spirited individuals met together to form an association for "the purpose of discovering, procuring, and preserving whatever may relate to the natural, civil, literary, and ecclesiastical history of the United States in general, and of this State in particular."

Such was and is the design of this Institution, as expressed in the original act of its incorporation, on the 10th of February, 1809; amended and continued in force by subsequent acts, and its charter, without limitation as to time, finally confirmed on the 2d of February, 1846, subject only to the usual restriction provided in all public acts.

During this semi-centennial existence, the Society has been without a permanent abode of its own; its treasures of historical materials were subjected to the injury of frequent removals, and liable at all times, in their insecure places of deposit, to be destroyed by fire. It has been a wanderer from place to place during these many years, but now, like the wayworn traveller, it has reached its home, and looks with pleased satisfaction on this abode for the various collections, gathered during these journeyings. Here it can display its various contributions, preserve its precious repository of the past, and make this library, with its constantly increasing additions, worthy of our city, State, and country.

The trustees, to whom the funds were confided for the construction of this fire-proof building, present themselves before you, on this interesting occasion, to report the disposition which has been made of these in the execution of their duties. From the incipient step in this enterprise, taken by the Society on the 1st of June, 1847, to its final consummation this day, a period of more than ten years has elapsed of continuous effort and varying solicitude. The Society had resolved upon a measure, for the attainment of which no means were provided, necessarily involving a large expenditure.

To collect and apply these means was an onerous undertaking, and could only be accomplished by strong, persevering, and well-directed efforts.

The trustees rejoice that it *is* accomplished, and that the hour has arrived when they can throw open the doors of this library for your reception, exhibit its collections, and tender to you their cordial congratulations on its final completion. A few small claims only remain yet to be paid, for the liquidation of which there is a sufficient fund reserved.

The five annual and the special reports, from time to time heretofore presented, exhibit the history of this enterprise and show the progress made in collecting funds; the difficulties encountered in the successsive attempts, and the successful effort finally accomplished in obtaining the requisite addition, which the liberal hearts of the liberal men of this great commercial city generously contributed.

It is not for those who now address you to speak of the architectural design of the building, of its style of decoration, or of the taste displayed in its exterior and interior appearance, and of the conveniences provided for the suitable arrangement of its numerous collections. They submit to the Society and the public these results; and if they meet their approbation, it will be a sufficient compensation for personal sacrifices and an honest endeavor to discharge faithfully their trust.

In the gallery specially set apart for the reception and preservation of the books and newspapers, and for their ready and convenient examination, these various collections are systematically arranged. In the apartment separately provided for our invaluable manuscripts, these unique treasures are similarly placed, where they can easily be referred to, and, to the greatest extent, secured from loss, depredation, or injury. Rising above these is the gallery devoted to the productions of art, which crowns, as it were, the whole. It contains the portraits of many men of our own land, who have made their names and their country illustrious by their talents and virtues; and evidences also of the genius of men like Cole, who have dignified the Arts of Design by the brilliant creations of their pencil.

The collections which comprise the printed and manuscript materials have been catalogued under the skilful care of our Librarian, and the Catalogue is now passing through the press.

There will also be a catalogue of the Gallery of Art; and it will furnish to the members a satisfactory estimate of the extent and richness of the entire collection.

On these extensive shelves, are placed, let us trust, in perpetual preservation, for the benefit of historical research, the proofs of those measures which led to the declaration of our country's independence; of the character of the men and their measures which achieved that independence; and of the causes and their effects, which are exhibited in the growth, power, resources, and extension of our Republic; stretching as it now does its giant limbs from ocean to ocean—from the regions of the hardy north to the genial climes of the sunny south. Its citizens have reached, in the march of empire, its western bound; and from thence look forth over the wide expanse of ocean to the opposite shores of Asia—prepared, when the hour arrives, to aid more fully in extending to that primal land of our race, the blessings and civilization of Christianity.

The earliest measure which occupied the attention of the trustees, was the appointment of its standing committees of finance, and on the building, and a treasurer of the fund. The duties which devolved upon that officer, and upon these several committees, the trustees are happy to have it in their power to say, have been most faithfully and zealously performed.

The committee to whom was committed the construction of the building, the preparation of the various contracts, the supervision of the work, and of the materials provided, and the expenditure of the fund, have with unremitted exertion, continued watchfulness, and great sacrifice of time and labor accomplished the results you this day witness.

They have made their final report to the trustees, from which it appears there have been, at various times and in different forms, expended for the site, twelve thousand and ninety-seven dollars and fifty-one cents; on the building, sixty-nine thousand four hundred and seven dollars and thirty cents, and for furnishing the same, three thousand two hundred and thirty-five dollars and three cents, making together an aggregate of eighty-four thousand seven hundred and thirty-nine dollars and eighty-four cents.

The details of these several items are set forth in the account current, annexed to and which forms part of their Report.

Thus it appears that the Building Fund has been sufficient to defray the expense of the site and of this edifice; leaving a balance to be applied to the furnishing of the building.

Persons not familiar with the difficulties of such an enterprise, executed under similar circumstances, cannot be aware of the unavoidable delays incident thereto. The procuring of a design for a fire-proof Library edifice, adapted to the uses and to meet in all respects the wishes of the Society, was a matter of great moment and careful consideration.

Then, the procuring of the contracts from responsible parties for the several departments into which the work divided itself, also occupied necessarily much care and preparation. The Committee in these matters were efficiently aided by the Architects, Messrs. Mettam and Burke, whose attention and vigilance were unremitted in guarding the interests of the Society, and advancing the work done.

The Committee state that it has been their endeavor, with the means at their disposal, to carry out the views of the trustees, and to accomplish the objects of the Society, in the highest degree practicable. Their constant aim has been to erect a building best suited to the purposes of the Society, creditable to its taste, and honorable to its patrons and the public. How far they have succeeded in this their constant and earnest endeavor, the Committee submit to the trustees, the Society, and the public.

If the committee on the building, to adopt their own language, "are so fortunate as to meet *their* approbation, they will feel amply compensated for all the effort, anxiety, and personal sacrifices, which a discharge of the duties devolved upon them has necessarily involved."

The Report of that committee is on file with the documents, to be preserved in grateful remembrance of its services, cheerfully given and faithfully executed.

It only remains, in this connection, for the trustees to add, that when the few debts yet to be paid are settled, and for the payment of which, as before stated, there is a fund in hand reserved, they will avail themselves of the earliest opportunity to communicate this desired result; and on that occasion submit their final Report, and surrender up the building, with its appurtenances, to the Society.

Cicero aptly termed Herodotus the "Father of History"—and History itself "the light of truth." Herodotus first gave to the world a general history adorned with the graces of a pure eloquence, and with that attractive simplicity, which was the prominent characteristic of all the more prominent of the most ancient authors.

His *Bust*, therefore, is properly placed above the portico which leads to these extensive galleries, repositories of facts, principles, and discoveries. From these may some congenial mind compose an "Historical Essay," which like that shall add to his own perpetual renown, and prove by his work the value, though less ambitious design, of our own.

The direct object of his work was to recount the victorious struggles of the Greeks with the Persians. But in tracing the causes of the events related, and in describing other nations connected with these events, he was led into the interesting and valuable digressions which constitute the remarkable portions of his book. It has been illustrated by the wisdom and matured experience of later ages; is confirmed in its material details by the learning of congenial minds; and abounds in a variety of information, touching the manners, customs, and national traits of which he speaks; and to which in many instances this highly distinguished author has furnished the only key of knowledge.

Thus, as an emblem of the objects which this Society has specially in view, this *Bust* proclaims from without to the passing inquirer the design of this *Historical Library*.

By the collections we are engaged in preserving and increasing, by every practicable measure, we are enlarging the means of historical inquiry and investigation, relating to the several departments classified in our Charter. In process of time this Library cannot fail to become better known and extensively consulted; and the just expectation may be indulged, that, by its intrinsic worth and amplitude of materials, it will become the great central resort for historical investigations of every kind, and give to our city and State the enviable distinction of possessing the best and most extensive Historical Library in this portion of the globe.

When Cicero was Quæstor in Sicily, his first object, on arriving there, was to visit the tomb of Archimedes. The officials of Syracuse, who waited upon him, being ignorant of its existence, he persevered in the search, which resulted in the discovery of the small column, hid by the surrounding undergrowth, on which, with great difficulty, was traced the almost illegible name of the great geometrician.

One hundred and thirty-six years had only elapsed since the Roman soldier slew the intellectual giant of Syracuse, whose dead body the Roman general entombed with honors becoming his genius. The simple inscription would have altogether perished, had not Cicero's admiration and perseverance made it immortal.

Little more than three quarters of a century have elapsed, and a citizen of these United States, in ardent admiration of the men who fell martyrs in the cause which made his country free and independent, might in vain seek for the places where some of these eminent patriots were interred! Already are many of these forgotten—nay, irrevocably obliterated! Over others the monumental stone has been placed, and the name of the illustrious dead inscribed on it; but, like the letters on the column of the world-renowned Syracusan—their names are almost effaced. Some patriot hand, like Old Mortality, must deepen with his chisel their almost obliterated inscriptions; some patriot pen, stirred by the incidents in the lives of these martyrs, perpetuate, by their biographies, the memory of their deeds; or, from these records around you, some gifted mind, touched with the sentiments which valor and worth never fail to create, must give to the world the knowledge and the benefit of their example.

The scholiast tells us, that when the friends of Pytheas, who had conquered in the Nemæan games, came to Pindar, with the request that he would write an ode on his victory, the poet demanded a sum which they refused to give. "We can have," say they, "a brazen statue for the money, which will be better than a poem." Changing their minds, however, they returned and offered him what he demanded. Upon this hint Pindar formed the graceful exordium, which has been thus elegantly translated:

"It is not mine, with forming hand,
To make a lifeless image stand
For ever on its base;
But fly, my verses, and proclaim
To distant lands, with deathless fame,
That Pytheas conquered in the rapid race!'

The poet's verse has proved more imperishable than a memorial ot brass! and the victor's triumph pales before the fire of genius, as mind rises triumphant over matter.

Here in this Library, the monument of the enterprise and liberality of Metropolitan New York, are contained the materials which testify to the growth, the power, and the extent of the country, and its natural resources and greatness. Here also are treasured up many celebrated works of her living sons, and testimonials of her honored dead. This Society enrolls in its list of members men eminently distinguished at the Bar, on the Bench, and in the Pulpit; also men of renown in the councils of the nation, and in our Congressional and Legislative Halls, and also of others well known to fame for their successful efforts in the several departments specified in our Charter.

She also numbers among her members the accomplished Historians of the United States and of this State, and also many whose genius, learning, and literary productions have added wreaths to the chaplet which adorns their native or adopted land. Among these shines, with the brilliancy of the "*Koh-i-noor*" among diamonds, the gifted author of the Sketch-Book, the varied productions of whose pen are as familiarly known as the sparkling wit, humor, and pathos with which they abound.

From these invaluable collections around you, some member of our Society, imbued with the spirit of the subject, may yet arise, like Herodotus, "to rescue from oblivion the memory of former incidents," yet untold; and "to render a just tribute to the many great and wonderful actions" of Americans, living and dead; whose names, though not as yet emblazoned on the records of History, are, however, enshrined in the hearts of their countrymen.

Yours is the monument, which we this evening dedicate, to the preservation and dissemination of Historic Truth. His will be the "deathless fame" of such an "Essay;" the best and an indelible inscription to commemorate fellow-members, your own incorporated Association.

By Order of the Trustees,

(Signed) FREDERIC DE PEYSTER,
Chairman.

NEW YORK, *Nov.* 3, 1857.

Dr. JOHN W. FRANCIS moved the acceptance of the report, which motion was seconded by Mr. BANCROFT, as follows:

## REMARKS OF MR. BANCROFT.

The Committee of Arrangements have assigned me the pleasing duty of seconding the motion for the acceptance of the Report. This beautiful and convenient building is the endowment for history made by the citizens and especially by the merchants of New York. It is their affectionate tribute in commemoration of the honorable fame of their ancestors, the varied fortunes of this great commonwealth, and that sympathy which binds the present generation with every generation of mankind that has gone before. Assembled here, we feel that events do not occur without adequate causes; that for every thing there is a reason; and that there are no gaps in the chain that connects the past with the present; that the institutions of to-day are but the necessary development of former time; that this moment in our existence, though often imperceptibly and in minute degrees, reflects light from all preceding ages. In an especial manner our own city and our own State have the most diversified affinities with ancient forms of civilization. The son of a merchant of the Venetian republic first ran down our coast. A fellow-citizen of Dante and Michael Angelo, under the banner of France, found out the channel into our harbor. When the fulness of time came for the establishment of a colony on this shore, Holland summoned Hudson from ranging among the jagged rocks of Spitzbergen and the icy mists of the Straits of Veigatz to lead the way in ascending our noble river; just as afterwards, when the great men of the age went forth, not like Titans to destroy, but with the better energies of creative power to lay the foundations of our Union, a Hamilton, whose cradle had been rocked by the breezes of the tropics, was called from the Antilles to plead for the adoption of the federal Constitution. Here assembled the first Congress of 1765; here the New York sons of liberty sent forth the first invitation for that of 1774; on our soil was won the decisive victory of independence, and here Washington inaugurated national freedom and union. The moment of planting the institutions of cultivated man within our limits was marked by whatever is most romantic in American history. The interior of the State was occupied by that wonderful people who had advanced furthest among savages in civil polity and confederations; and while all that was most daring in adventure, all that was most self-sacrificing in religion, were entering on the one side with Champlain and the Catholic missions; on the other, the great commercial republic of Europe, the forerunner and fostering example for America, was preparing to take possession of Albany and Manhattan. In the Old World, republican government has fallen on evil days—and a kingdom has taken the place of the glorious Dutch union of sovereign states. But if the living waters of freedom have diminished in that European land, through which they once flowed most brightly, they are but as the fountain of Arethusa, which disappears only to gush forth again in a happier clime. America claims a share of the honors due to Chaucer, and Raleigh, and Shakspeare—the English literature that preceded the first planting of Virginia. The glory of the Dutch republic is peculiarly our inheritance. The republican liberty of the Netherlands, which was vindicated by a contest longer and more trying than that of Athens with Persia, is to be found only here. It is ours, all ours. The banks of the Hudson are its asylum, where it renews its perennial youth like the eagle. The gift of this building has another significance; it is one of many proofs that the busiest city is the most genial home for literature. Where there is the most action, there there must be the most thought. The world of the scholar and the world of the man of affairs are all one. The widest connections furnish the greatest opportunity of concentrating knowledge, and the readiest means for its diffusion. In such a community there is no possibility of a dead calm, of a stagnation of mind. The ever-moving winds of controversy winnow opinions, and the fire of truth is kept alive and fed by contributions from all climes. And what city is bound by more associations and ties to all parts of the world than our New York? At one moment one of its sons discovers the Antarctic continent; at another, a ship from our wharves is planted by a man of heroic mould, illustrious in his youth,—the immortal Kane,—among the icebergs of Greenland, as the imperishable monument that of all the flags in the world the stars and stripes have approached nearest to the pole. But if we would see the intimate connection of our city with every part of the globe and the many nations of the earth, we have only to look about us, not at the magazines of our merchants, where, indeed, every thing is gathered together from ocean and from land for the support, the comfort, and the grace of life, but at the men moving in our streets, representing as they do not our own country only, not England and Holland only, but every nation of Europe from Cadiz to Warsaw, from Ireland to the Isles of Greece; so that by necessity the civilization of all those lands is intertwined with ours. The seers who look into futurity abound in their eulogies of the coming commercial greatness of New York, when its proportion of the mercantile marine shall be still greater than it is now, and it shall be the centre of the exchanges of the world; when its population shall fill this island, and, like a branching vine, cover all the lands around. But this superiority in material resources is not enough; the crowning glory of New York must be its advancement in intelligence. Here must flourish unsurpassed colleges of that science of which the blessed skill removes disease, or charms away its pains. Here we must have schools of jurisprudence to teach it as a science, resting on immutable principles of justice, to interpret international and constitutional law on a system that shall be at once cosmopolitan and national, breathing union among ourselves and good will to all the peoples of the earth. Here where the crowded streets show the most of that favored being who alone was created in the image of his Maker, the truths that lift man above the vicissitudes of time, and connect him with things that are eternal, must shine out in their purest lustre. Here divine art must make visible to the senses the forms of beauty that repose in the capacious recesses of creative genius. Here universities must gather together all the fountains of truth and send the living waters through the land. Let the comprehensive and liberal spirit of our merchants and the vivifying intelligence of scholars join together to promote the fullest development of every capacity for good. This edifice is an earnest of that co-operation.

President KING, of Columbia College, then addressed the President as follows:

### REMARKS OF PRESIDENT KING.

Mr. President: The scene presented here this evening carries me back to other days—I may say to other generations; and looking round upon the few scattered ancients, my contemporaries, among the large assemblage of younger men, the active, stirring men of this active, stirring age, it may be said, almost without a figure, that posterity is here to welcome and to encourage the early friends of the Historical Society who yet survive to witness, and take part in, this joyous and most gratifying inauguration of a building not unworthy of the treasures it is to contain, and which it is to secure against the danger irreparable for such a library and collection as ours—of fire.

I thank you, Mr. President, and the gentlemen of the Committee of Invitation, for giving me this opportunity of being present at such a festival, and taking a part, however humble, in its proceedings.

Born in the city of New York, I have always felt the full force of the exalting claim of the Apostle of the Gentiles, that he was "a citizen of no mean city;" and whatever tends to promote the honor or add to the illustrious annals of the city or State, enlists my earnest sympathy and co-operation.

And in illustrious annals there is no State in our wide Union that surpasses New York, and not one that with so much to say, has said so little in her own behalf.

But there are laid up here, sir, and will, I would fain hope, continue to be laid up, treasures of private letters, diaries, and memoirs, which together with the printed materials accessible to all, will furnish authentic matter for that history of New York which is yet to be written.

We need at this day, especially, to popularize the study of our history, and especially of our own history; for, diligently and honestly pursued, it is the *essential* study among a people where all are called to take a part in public affairs, to make either the laws or those who do make them. In this study they will perceive that however oppression and wrong may for a time prosper, the Nemesis of History follows close upon the guilty career, and brands with indelible infamy the bold, bad man, who would "owe his greatness to his country's ruin."

Men, indeed, of the school of Sir Robert Walpole, whose whole statecraft consists in the one sordid maxim—false as it is sordid—"every man has his price," may sneer at history as a tissue of lies, and seek to throw doubt upon all acts and all motives that cannot be traced to the unscrupulous theory of their statesmanship; but the memorials which such a Society as ours gathers, preserves, and finally publishes, refute this degrading hypothesis—memorials of private letters never designed for the light, and of conversations held in the intimacy and privacy of home, revealing the heart of the speaker or writer, letters and memoirs such as constitute the matchless collection which Sparks has given us of our great Washington. How few the men that ever lived who, acting on so great a theatre, could stand the ordeal of such an honest publication. Yet who that has ever read these letters but feels that, however exalted before may have been his admiration of Washington, it is enhanced by these volumes.

So, too, we have already manuscript treasures inedited, and having now a repository safe from the destroying fire, and placed beyond the possibility of what once was a scarcely less threatening danger—the sheriff's hammer—we may reasonably calculate to have many more precious family papers, records, and memorials confided to us, which though they may not illustrate such names as Washington or Jay, rarely, and only at long intervals vouchsafed to any nation, shall yet teach the coming ages that God, and therefore Truth, is in History, and Virtue and

Patriotism in public men. It is a great trust to be the depository of such materials; what we see before us is the sure warrant that the trust is well reposed, and will be faithfully fulfilled.

Rev. Dr. WILLIAM ADAMS, being called upon, responded as follows:

REMARKS OF REV. DOCTOR ADAMS.

I am somewhat startled, Mr. President, at the formality of your call, at this stage of the proceedings, since I had entered the hall with the expectation of being a listener, rather than a speaker. I had, indeed, passed my word that I would be present, and that if the occasion should require, I would say a word, by meeting any necessity of the case; but I must confess that the bait which lured me into this hall was the expectation of listening to the distinguished speakers of the evening, especially the promise of hearing Mr. Irving, and Mr. Verplanck, the original founders of this Society.

The researches of the antiquary and the labors of the historian have always, with minds of a certain order, been the theme of satire. Even such a man as Dr. JOHNSON confessed to no patience with history. He would not even read the elaborate works of HUME and ROBERTSON; and on one occasion he positively forbade Mr. BOSWELL ever to mention in his presence again the Punic War. He ridiculed BEAUCLERC, and other members of the Kit-Cat Club, for what they reported as having seen in foreign travel. Yet the mind of Dr. JOHNSON was precisely of that order which would have been benefited by the more copious induction of facts derived from history and travel. How different was it with Dr. PALEY, who, with his bob-wig and round hat, was the very impersonation of *bonhommie*,—who requested a friend, when going upon foreign travel, to bring back, he cared not how common a thing, "if it was nothing but an old shoe, or an old smock," which would illustrate the manners and condition of a people.

After all that we say of the dignity of history, it is the small, the common, and the humble, which give us a correct idea of existing society. No better illustration of this can be afforded than the letters of Dr. JOHNSON to Mrs. THRALE. In his letters from the Hebrides, we have a perfect picture of the manners of that isolated people. We see the very things that they eat, their dirty habits, the comfortless apartments in which they slept; and it seems now to have gleamed upon the mind of that old man himself, that it might have been better for him if, at an earlier period of his life, he had not been so restricted to the habits of Englishmen, and that he had himself given more attention to history and foreign travel.

A little incident like the advertisement in a paper, than which nothing can be more common or insignificant, may give to us a correct illustration of the state of society. In our own archives there is a file of the *Boston News-Letter*, the oldest newspaper published upon this continent. Cast your eye over its pages, and you will be convinced that that smutty chronicle is the index of the greatest revolutions of Providence. On the 13th of November, 1732, you find an advertisement which reads as follows:

"This day, at 4 o'clock, will be sold at public vendue, at the Sun Tavern, a parcel of red and blue muslins, perpets, and threads, for the Guinea Trade. Also, three or four very likely negroes, just arrived. All to be seen at the place of sale."

The African slave trade in the city of Boston, a little more than one century ago! A good thing would it be for us to be more familiar with these historic facts, that we may sprinkle our fervor with a little cool patience. Shem, Ham, and Japhet, instead of pelting one another with mutual recriminations, would do well to consult those earlier facts of history, and, with forbearance and sympathy, cast the mantle of charity over the nakedness of our common ancestors.

Ask any intelligent traveller, returning from the Old to the New World, what are those objects which have awakened in his mind the greatest interest, and he will inform you, not always those things which are regarded great and noble in the judgment of common men, so much as those things, often simple, humble, and insignificant in themselves, which stand related to the great discoveries of science, the great achievements of liberty, and the general progress of the human race; not always those stupendous piles of architecture, whose grandeur and decorations have exhausted the wealth of centuries; not always the sceptres and crowns and regalia of kings, which have been worn often by men and women whom no gold or gems could adorn; not so much the abbeys and cathedrals, in whose long and solemn aisles repose the ashes of the mighty dead—the few good among the many bad. He will tell you of such things as the cottage near the city of Genoa, the birth-place of Christopher Columbus, on the front of which is inscribed these words:

"Unus erat mundus; duo sint, ait iste:—fuere."

"There was one world—there may be two," said he. It is the house of Galileo, at Florence, containing his scientific implements, and among them that little Dutch telescope, with which this great "Columbus of the Heavens," as he has been called, made his first researches in the firmament. It is the little lamp which still hangs in the Cathedral at Pisa, the oscillation of which first put in motion the mind of that great philosopher concerning the laws of the pendulum and the measurement of time. It is the pulpit of John Knox, in the Antiquary's Hall at Edinburgh,—plain, stout, and oaken,—in which that noble reformer thundered out his denunciations against religious despotism; and by the side of it, the stool which Jennie Geddes flung at the head of the Dean of Edinboro', when, lending himself a tool to royal oppression, he dared to curtail the liberty of worship in God's people—a singular projectile, but the signal shot of a great revolution! It is that little bit of plaster in one of the cells of the Tower of London, which you cannot read but with a suffused eye, on which are scratched, as with a nail, by some noble martyr for the truth, these verses of scripture:

"Be thou faithful unto death, and I will give thee a crown of life. He that continueth unto the end, the same shall be saved."

It is the little Latin Bible belonging to Martin Luther inscribed all over with marginal notes, in the handwriting of that great Reformer, brought by Gustavus Vasa, and now in the Royal Museum of Stockholm, the lever by which in his own lifetime that stalwart hero prised up fifty millions of people to light and liberty.

Those are the things which are truly great, though small in themselves, because they are associated in every mind with the progress of the human race in knowledge and in freedom.

If there be importance attached to such objects in foreign lands, how much more important are similar objects in our own. A collection of newspapers, of pamphlets, orations, sermons, may be regarded in themselves as entirely valueless; but they serve to preserve to us a perfect picture of times that are past, more faithful often than the largest folios.

We have all been under the impression that injustice has been done to many of the events and personages of American history, through the prejudice of foreign historians. No better illustration can we have than the different feelings which prevail in regard to two distinguished parties who figured during the American Revolution upon opposite sides of that great contest—Major André of the British army, and Captain Hale, of our own. What man, woman, or child that ever read the touching fate of André, who has not been moved to a genial sympathy? Gallant, educated, accomplished, he met the fate of a soldier, amid the tears of those who executed him. How few are acquainted with the history and the fate of Capt. Hale! Educated at Yale College, accomplished in person and manners, high in the confidence of his military superiors, he volunteered to accomplish a nobler service than his British contemporary, and met his fate with a nobler self-possession and courage. Requesting writing materials on the morning of his execution, that he might address a farewell line to his mother and sisters, he was denied that facility by the provost of the British army, who said that he "did not intend the rebels should ever know that they had so brave a man in their body;" and when he saw the fatal gallows erected, here in Chambers-street of our own city, instead of flinching, he said his only regret was that he had not more than one life to lay down for the good of his country. Yet no Metropolitan monument is reared to his honor on the spot where he fell, though the remains of André sleep beneath sculptured marble in Westminster Abbey.

It is a pious duty devolving upon us, to render justice to the deeds of our fathers. Let us dig up their statues from the sand and rubbish where they have fallen, and place them upon their proper pedestals: Hamilton in Wall street; the incorruptible Jay in our City Hall; all the civil and military heroes of our annals: let us study their calm and serious features, and copy whatever was noble or good in their example.

However it may be with other people, we are the last who can afford to forego the advantage of antiquarian and historical research. It was a remark made by Dr. Chalmers:—"One thing I should not like in America: I should not like your *raw and recent* population. I love to feel, when I am walking here in Edinboro', that I am treading on the *same stanes* with my ancestors."

In breaking away from the old world, tearing ourselves from the old universities, from those ancient parks,

"With their sylvan honors of feudal bark,"

with all that has been consecrated by the lapse of time—we are in danger of losing our reverence for that which is old, and attaching ourselves exclusively to that which is new. Ours, indeed, is not a recent history. Most cordially do I sympathize with the remark made by the accomplished historian and orator (Mr. Bancroft), who has preceded me, that we have an indefeasible claim in all of British life and history. We have not lost our pedigree by being translated across the sea. There is no bend of illegitimacy in our national escutcheon. The fame of Milton and Spenser and Shakspeare belongs to us as much as to any

Englishman. They who still retain possession of the ancestral isle have no prescriptive claim to those crown jewels of English literature. Their blood is our own. Nevertheless, we do well to guard ourselves against those influences that might affect us, from familiarity with that which is recent and novel. Let us reverently regard whatever is old, and fixed, and stable. Let us not swing loose from the anchorage of historic association. Rather let us cultivate that wisdom which, forming an accurate judgment of the past, and a correct horoscope of the present, shall forecast those noble anticipations of the future which are nurtured alike by our history and our religious faith.

Rev. GEORGE W. BETHUNE, D. D., also addressed the Society, and the Report of the Trustees was accepted.

BENJAMIN ROBERT WINTHROP, Esq., then, at the request of the President, read the letter accompanying his donation to the Society of the "Washington Chair," which was accepted, with the thanks of the Society.

The President announced that the Fifty-Third Anniversary of the Society would be celebrated at the Library, on Tuesday evening, November 17th, when the Address would be delivered by JOHN W. FRANCIS, M. D., LL. D.

The President also announced that the Library and Galleries would be open for the reception of the families of members on the following evening, Wednesday, November 4th.

The benediction was then pronounced by Rev. PETER S. VAN PELT, D. D.

---

On Wednesday evening, November 4th, pursuant to the announcement of the President, there was a very large attendance of members accompanied by their families at the Library. About 9 o'clock, the company having assembled in the Lecture Room, the President took the chair, and introduced the Rev. Dr. OSGOOD, who addressed them as follows:

### REMARKS OF DR. OSGOOD ON THE DOMESTIC ASPECTS OF HISTORY.

Dr. OSGOOD, on being introduced by the President, remarked, that the assembly met now to complete the last evening's dedication, and that the Society came now with their families to say Amen to the consecrating prayer, and to take possession of this new literary home. The present occasion seemed to him to be peculiarly of a domestic character; and his words would aim to illustrate the worth of History as a record of Humanity, in its affections as well as its politics, and in its relations to woman as well as to man. He was not sorry to address an audience so richly representing the true humanity; and he did not consider an audience of men alone to be wholly human; and perhaps he might presume to say that an audience of women alone was no much nearer the complete humanity which God created in his own image, when "male and female created he them."

He then invited the ladies and gentlemen present to survey with him the various apartments of the edifice, in a passing review, and to interpret the building itself as the symbol of the historical creed of the Society.

I. Begin with the Refectory, and interpret it as a symbol of sociality in its literary relations. The table surely has an historical significance; and it needed no great antiquarian learning to prove that eating and drinking were very ancient institutions, and were likely to survive the wreck of empires, and the changes of fashions. With the progress of civilization, the table rises in dignity; and the natural appetite, to which it appeals, is refined and exalted by the intellectual and social tastes that are concentrated and nurtured by its cheerful plenty. The Refectory is in the basement of our edifice; and its position teaches the fact that agriculture, with its daily bread, is the material basis of human welfare, and that our bread is twice blessed when partaken in generous fellowship. Our bread is never truly blessed unless womanly grace smiles upon it; and here to-night, with our wives, daughters, and friends, we accept the Refectory as the symbol of our sociality.

II. Ascend a story of the edifice, and we enter this spacious and convenient Lecture Room, which marks the intention of the Society to be an instrument of popular education. Here history is to be presented, not as the interest of a few antiquarian scholars, as dry as the dust on their folios, but as the interest of our common humanity, as a study for all rational creatures, for youth and age, scholar and merchant, for woman and for man. Here our monthly meetings are to be held, and our regular historical papers are to be read. It might, perhaps, be expected that the more various, and especially the feminine elements in the audience, would act favorably upon the manner and matter of the speaking and reading; and that bright eyes, with their quick intuition, would drive all dulness from the rostrum, as sunshine drives away the clouds. But it must be understood that order was to be preserved, without respect of persons; and that our President, who could shine in parlors as well as Senates, was quite as much master of the art of winning gentle volatility to sobriety by his bland dignity, as of subduing unruly men to order by his manly authority. In all soberness, it is to be hoped that this hall of audience will be one of the educational institutions of the city.

III. The Library is our symbol of history, as literature, and of literature, in all its compass, as the record of the affections as well as of the understanding. History has been too often poorly interpreted into a register of dates, upon a tomb of relics of the dead. It should be regarded as the record of human life in all its compass; and our new library, with its admirable arrangements, and large hospitality, fitly expresses this idea. It is well that the Library is open to woman as well as to man; and this fact will tend to give a truer expression to our historical treasures, and show, ere long, what dry antiquarians have too often forgotten, that there is a line of white ribbon as well as of red tape running through the looms of time. We have, on our front wall, the head of Herodotus, the father of history. Where is the mother of history, or is there none? Who is that fair head over our vestibule, the lovely woman with a star for her diadem? Is it a type of our America with her vesper star, or is it Memory with her twilight retrospections, or is it the ideal Mother of History, of whom every true womanly soul is the loyal daughter, even as the nine muses of old were daughters of Mnemosyne?

IV. The Picture Gallery crowns the edifice, and presents the beautiful arts as the flower of human civilization. Why wonder at the arrangement? Why speak as if the beautiful were the lying paint on the cheek of meretricious Folly, instead of the healthful bloom on the face of Truth, that fair daughter of the Eternal Mind? Art, too, like literature, is rooted in the affections, and has its domestic side and its feminine inspirations. If few women are comparatively artists, and no woman has ever given a masterpiece of the first class to sculpture or painting, or to music, or eloquence, or poetry, the balance is made up, and more too, by the fact that the masterpieces of men have, for the most part, been inspired by women, and that, as with DANTE, so with most great artists, woman is man's Beatrice, the genius of his inspirations.

Mention was here made of the worth of the beautiful arts to human welfare; and it was said that as the French naturalist, ADANSON, asked in his will that a wreath made of the fifty-eight classes of plants which he had established by his own researches might be laid upon his coffin; so we have laid upon this, not tomb, but temple of history, a garland of flowers of art, whose enlivening and healing grace shall be the blessing of generations to come. COLE's Course of Empire was spoken of, and the artist was called the EDMUND SPENSER of American art.

The address, which was nearly an hour long, and is here presented only in outline, closed with some reference to the fitness of the season for the opening of this edifice. At this time of commercial depression, it was good for us to think of the old times of trial, and strengthen our too effeminate manners by a little of the ancient manliness under misfortune. Read the year '57 backwards, and it is '75, and speaks to us of the school of Revolutionary heroes. In this dark time, we light up this beautiful hall of history, and in the cheering ray we brighten all sclemn remembrances with the radiance of cheerful and progressive hopes.

After some remarks by Gen. PROSPER M. WETMORE, the company retired.

www.ingramcontent.com/pod-product-compliance
Lightning Source LLC
LaVergne TN
LVHW010831120826
845149LV00016B/640

* 9 7 8 1 4 1 8 1 8 7 6 5 1 *